Already Awake

Already Awake

dialogues with
Nathan Gill

NON-DUALITY PRESS

Acknowledgements

Heartfelt gratitude to Eddie Carmichael for his dedication and diligence in transcribing all the talks and to Rose Youd for editorial comment and proofreading.

Non-Duality Press

6 Folkestone Road Salisbury SP2 8JP United Kingdom
www.non-dualitybooks.com

Copyright © Nathan Gill 2004

First Printing September 2004
Revised edition July 2006

ISBN 0-9547792-2-3

To Amy & Lucy

Contents

Preface

Since the original appearance of *Clarity* as an intro-
duction to the talks, there have been numerous
requests for further written material. As the talks are
the arena for this particular expression, it seems fit-
ting that *Already Awake* should appear in the form of
distillations from transcripts of recorded dialogues
with groups and individuals.

Although clarity remains the same—there is never
'more' clarity—there is a natural evolution in its
expression, and so it feels appropriate that a revised
version of *Clarity* should introduce the main part of
this book.

It is the delight of the play that Consciousness
appears as everything and is only ever pointing to and
delighting in itself.

Nathan Gill
September 2004

Clarity

The Story

I was born in 1960 into a working-class family in South-East England.

As a child I was intense and inquisitive—hours spent reading adventure and mystery books, hobbies which involved searching for antique artefacts, long treks into the countryside at every opportunity. Seeking began at an early age!

As I grew up, my restlessness led to difficulties in choosing a career, an inability to focus in any particular area. I left school as early as I could, decided to train as a chef, and then ended up working on construction sites.

I enjoyed this very much. It absorbed much of my restless energy and required no investment of responsibility. I took my orders and got on with the work—leaving me free to indulge in roaming in the thought story.

There was a constant interest in the mysteries of the body and the universe—experimenting with various diets and herbal treatments, looking at the stars, eating magic mushrooms, and pushing the body to the limit with weight-training and body-building.

In my early twenties I was forced to slow down. A shoulder injury brought the weight-training to an end, my wife gave birth to our first daughter when I was twenty-two, and I changed from construction to horticulture. For several years I picked fruit in Kent orchards from early summer to late autumn and gardened at other times of the year. During this period my thoughts turned to spiritual and esoteric matters.

Around 1985 I joined a fraternal order which sent me regular monthly lessons in mysticism and 'universal law'. I enjoyed doing experiments and reading monographs each week.

After a couple of years I became interested in the teachings of a deceased Indian teacher, offered in monthly lessons and incorporating a guru-disciple relationship—even though the guru was already dead! I took this up and became involved with seeking enlightenment. This was my new obsession.

Another couple of years and several spiritual techniques later, I grew bored with it and happened upon a book by a western guru. This book told me that I was already awake and needed no liberation. The truth of what he was saying seemed obvious. However, he then went on (in the next few years and over the course of quite a few books) to proclaim himself the world teacher and offered a guru-disciple relationship for those who were interested.

Well, this time I was having none of it, although over the following five years I read a few more of his books as well as just about every other spiritual book I could get my hands on. But nothing really cut it for me the way the western guru's original book had done. Somewhere in me I knew it was true that I was already awake and free, but I was still confused, because I seemed to be just an ordinary person with all the usual sorts of problems that ordinary people have.

Anyway, I got sick of this guy's teachings and all the more traditional spiritual stuff, and next I hit the

Advaita scene. I read everything by and about all the big Advaita names.

A lot of the confusion that I had felt before dissolved. I understood that all there is is Consciousness. So why did I still feel like a separate 'me'? What was the missing link? If I was already awake and free, then why did my life often seem like a pile of dung?

In 1997 I read Tony Parsons' first book, *The Open Secret*. I contacted him and he invited me to join a discussion at a house in London. It soon became clear to me how much mystique I had built around the whole 'enlightenment' drama. Tony appeared as an ordinary man and spoke with humour and patience. I listened to what he said in response to people's questions and I was struck by the simplicity of his answers. I went to more discussions over the next year and spoke to Tony on the phone when I could.

I wanted to make him into my 'teacher', but he explained that he had nothing to teach, and simply pointed out that there is only Consciousness—which I already am. Although I had understood this to some extent already, now it really began to sink in.

Tony pointed out that there does not need to be any kind of 'event' associated with the recognition of our true nature. Well, as it happened, in September 1998 an event arose. I was gardening and the rain was drizzling down. I looked up, and there was a subtle sense of 'me' not being there. I got on my bike and cycled around the lanes and it seemed as though there was a movie going on, without any effort necessary on my part to be taking part in it.

With this sudden dropping of the 'I', all need

for understanding fell away. Even though Tony had pointed out that an event is not necessarily associated with the recognition of our nature as Consciousness, I had obviously still been subtly waiting for one, because now that this event or experience was occurring, it was seen as 'permission to be awake'. Without realising, I had been waiting for a confirmation of my true nature.

I rang Tony and excitedly explained what was going on and, with this new 'permission to be awake', speaking arose from clarity rather than the point of view of 'I'. Tony recognised that I was no longer relating to him as a separate character who was trying to get something, ie from the point of view of seeking and understanding.

As the day wore on, the mesmerisation as 'I' began subtly to return and claim this event—which was precisely the absence of 'I'—as 'my' enlightenment, 'my' awakening. There was a focus on the sense of sudden release—a blissfulness that arose in the absence of the 'I'—as being the enlightenment I had waited for.

I woke the next day. Was it still there? Yes! Then, after a few days, I noticed that the sense of release was wearing off a bit—but a couple of days later it was full on again. After a couple of weeks of it coming and going and of the 'I' reappearing and trying to hold on to its own absence, I went to one of Tony's discussions and the blissfulness seemed to be re-charged through being there. But then a few days later it disappeared altogether and there was mesmerisation as the 'I' again. I didn't say anything about it to Tony and I didn't go to the meetings for a while. I felt confused.

Then I read a book by a woman who described an absence of the 'I' which lasted many years. After some time, she was told by certain 'teachers' that this was enlightenment. Then she became ill and died, and, in the afterword to her book, written by a friend of hers, I read that near the end she became confused and frustrated because the event had disappeared and the 'I' had returned.

Suddenly it became clear that these events where the 'I' suddenly disappears can actually be very confusing, so far as clarity is concerned. Such an event may last a few seconds or ten years or more, but unless the 'I' is seen for what it is—as simply a thought—then when this 'I' returns, there is a sense of loss, a sense of confinement in being an identified character again. As the identified character, the desire arises for more of this 'enlightenment', and there is the sense of being back in the agitation and tension of the play of seeking.

Now it was seen that all of life is a great play. There is only ever *knowing,* but this knowing is seemingly veiled by the mesmerisation with the 'I' thought and all the other thoughts that appear as 'my' story. Our true nature as Consciousness is awareness *and* the appearances. The 'I' is simply a part of the scenery, as are all the other various images, and when it is seen through—or seen for what it is—then seeking and tension fall naturally away.

It was clear also that this seeing through the 'I' is not necessarily a sudden happening, but may appear to happen gradually, as part of the play of life. And rather than in a rush of blissfulness, the natural ease of being is gently, gradually revealed.

The confusion was gone. I no longer required any event or sudden dropping of the 'I' to prove my nature as Consciousness. It was clear that the whole of my life and 'spiritual' search was arising as a play in Consciousness, and I understood the confusion around this whole issue, why 'spirituality' and 'enlightenment' are confused with simple clarity. This recognition of my true nature was not associated with any kind of event. It was clear that an event of any kind is easily confusing if it occurs without clarity—which is the seeing through of the 'I' and the thought story.

Obviously the event that happened in the garden was of no particular significance, nor is any other event. The occurrence of the event merely brought my confusion to a head and allowed the clear seeing of how I had been subtly waiting for an event as 'permission' to be what I already am. This clarity is not dependent on the absence or presence of the 'I'. If the 'I' appears, it is simply seen for what it is.

To bring this little story to a close: during the years of spiritual seeking I was divorced, married and divorced again, a single parent to my two daughters throughout most of their school years. I settled in a small village in Kent with not so robust physical health, and until recently worked locally as a gardener. Life is presently quiet and simple.

Consciousness

You are Consciousness, oneness, all that *is*, the source and appearance of all. All appearances rise and fall in awareness, nothing else is ever happening. People are passing, clouds are going by, conversations are going on, thoughts appear and disappear. All unfolds presently in awareness.

This appearance as the character is already the perfect expression of oneness—nothing needs to change for this to be so. No awakening or enlightenment is needed—all of this is simply the story in the play. There is only already awakeness as oneness, regardless of whether there is mesmerisation with the play of images, or resting in recognition as your true nature.

This present appearance, however ordinary or extraordinary, is the content of awareness. Awareness and content are one—Consciousness. *You* are Consciousness—awake and aware and presently appearing as everything.

The Play of Life

Seen in clarity, life appears as a great play. You—
Consciousness—play all the roles and it is part of the
play that You usually play the roles without knowing
Your real identity. But sometimes, as part of the show,
there is recognition of Your true nature.

When there is involvement as a character in the
play without recognition of Your true nature the role
is taken seriously and all the dramas of life seemingly
appear from this. If a role is played where there is recognition of Your true nature, the play is seen for what
it is.

When Your true nature becomes obvious, the
character doesn't disappear in a flash of light, nor put
on ochre robes and have disciples, nor teach 'spiritual'
truths—although any of these is possible, depending
on the pattern of the character's role in the play. The
character will likely appear as he or she did before
recognition. The character is likely to continue to
lead what is an ordinary life in the play. It is not even
necessarily so that the character tells anyone or com-
municates what is now obvious.

The whole play has no purpose or point beyond
present appearance. It is Your cosmic entertainment.
You are Your play. It has no existence separate from
You.

Life As It Is

When the whole conceptual story of a life extended in thought beyond the present content of awareness is no longer seriously entertained, there is a natural relaxing into ease. Identification as the 'I', or psychological self-sense, is merely an appearance in awareness, an addition to the appearance of the body image.

The allowing of life as it is—rather than any efforts to be rid of thought or 'I', or to become 'enlightened'—allows seeking to fall naturally away. Within the play, all efforts to be rid of 'I' merely reinforce identification with it.

Resting in life as it is does not bring ordinary bodily life to an end in some magical firework display of enlightenment. Thought continues to arise, life carries on, but it is no longer burdened by the complication of the search for unity. Life is seen as the expression *of* wholeness, rather than as a search *for* it.

You are Consciousness. Whatever Your present appearance, it is already perfect, including any play of identification as 'I', and also any seeking to be rid of 'I'. Life as the character is simply the play of appearances in awareness and has no requirement for awakening. There is only already awakeness.

Spiritual Life

Spiritual life has no particular relevance to clarity—it is simply part of the play of life. But because of what appears in the play as the individual's evolution through progressively 'higher' or finer stages of life, it is confused as a prerequisite to clarity.

The ordinary character, occupied with all the usual affairs of human life, perhaps becomes interested in religion or self-improvement. There could be a movement towards seeking enlightenment and maybe an interest in non-duality.

But this progression is not necessary for clarity to appear. Clarity could appear at any time in any character in the play. None of the apparent stages in the play of life has any ability to produce clarity. Advaitic knowledge has no more a special ability to create a condition for clarity to appear than does any other part of the play.

Spiritual life is based on the presumption of individuality, with reunion with the whole as the projected goal. And as a means to achieve this goal of reunion, an array of exotic techniques and methods are provided in the play, to 'purify' the individual, to get rid of the 'I', to become enlightened, etc.

The fundamental point that is missed at every stage of the individual's quest is that the individual—being played by You, who are Consciousness—is already what he or she is seeking. Nothing can make the seeker any more what he or she already is.

The search and all the methods and techniques employed are there for no more reason than any other part of the play. They arise for their own sake, simply as part of the play.

Clarity requires no spiritual 'qualifications'. Consciousness in the form of a person sitting in a lotus posture, visualising a purple light in their genitals, breathing the universe into the solar plexus, chanting om and ascending up the spine into the thousand-petalled lotus, has no greater chance of reunion than does Consciousness in the form of a drug addict in a ghetto. Consciousness is already perfectly present in either case, so reunion is neither necessary nor possible.

Spiritual life imposes many conditions on the 'impure' and 'separate' individual—special meditations, appropriate behaviours, ceremonies, diets, sexual conduct, destruction of the ego, cessation of thought, finding the stillness, surrendering to the guru, etc.

Consciousness, already being Consciousness in whatever form it appears, has no need of a vegetarian diet, celibacy, tantric sexuality, meditation or gurus. Consciousness is already all of these things. If there is a liking for chanting, meditation, eating vegetarian food or practising tantric sex, then that's all fine. But it won't help the recognition of this which You already are.

The character's attention could move to exotic planes and realms—see the continual creation and dissolution of the universe at the atomic level and experience the eternal ecstatic cosmic union of Siva and Shakti. But when you get back, don't forget to go to work on Monday, pay the electricity bill and clean the toilet!

You—Consciousness—also appear in Your play as individuals playing the roles of teachers, masters or gurus. In some cases there may have been or there may be still occurring a transcendental event, which the individual believes is his or her 'enlightenment'. If the individual was already following a guru or a certain teaching before the event, it is likely that the beliefs and methods that appeared to lead up to the event will now be passed on to the individual's followers as 'the truth'.

As part of the play, some of these 'teachers' may even have the ability to induce unusual experiences in the disciple via energy transmission—often a strong attraction for the disciple.

There is nothing wrong with any of this. All of it is the perfection of the play. Carry on with it. Have fun. None of it leads to clarity.

I Am That, but ...

I Am That, but ... I need to take responsibility, heal my life, go deeper, become more aware, be here now, enter the stillness, save the planet, express my emotions, think positively, become the witness, be blissful, find a guru, be useful, find the meaning of life, calm my thoughts, do good works, get rid of the ego, enter manhood or womanhood, be more practical, get enlightened, find my soul-mate, perform a ceremony, become initiated, get in touch with my feelings ...

Maybe you do. How can I disagree? While you're busy with all that, I'll go and have a cup of tea and read the paper.

What Already Is

What is, right now, is perfection—presence has not arisen from the past and is not leading to the future. All appears presently as a play in awareness.

The apparently separate individual may be involved with self-improvement, spiritual life or anything else throughout the unfolding of that life. But only the clarity of what You really are undermines the search for awakening or for being anything other than what already is.

The Obvious

The play of life is not a separate creation watched and presided over by You. You—Consciousness—appear presently as the play, already wide awake, unable therefore to awaken. You are always obvious to Yourself; never hidden.

The characters in the play have no separate existence, only an apparent one. The characters are You celebrating Yourself, immersed in the great play of life, playing the game of looking for Yourself, sometimes recognising Yourself within and as the appearance of Your play.

This communication about clarity has no particular relevance or significance over any other part of the play. It carries no merit and has no point. There is no purpose for You to find Yourself.

With clarity, all of this is made obvious—Your present appearance as the play in all its myriad forms, the recognition of the non-necessity of everything. Right now You are Consciousness, appearing as a character in Your play. Maybe You think You need confirmation. Forget it. Relax. You already are That.

With much love to You from Yourself.

Afterword

What has been sought all along is found to be none other than this which is the seeking. The ultimate goal or prize turns out to be what already is. There is nothing and no one to find. There is awareness with no one being aware. All along You have been the butt of Your own cosmic joke. The magnificence of all appearances, everywhere you look and seek is simply Your own play or dream of being. There is nothing and no one and yet there is awareness whereby everything appears, including this appearance as an ordinary man or woman. You are, and always have been, completely awake, aware and present, but merely mesmerised by Your own cosmic play.

The character, Nathan, sought enlightenment as an escape from what appeared as the problems, trials and boredom of ordinary life. The ordinary life continues but no longer in distraction from presence. The search for the extraordinary is over—life is as it is.

SUMMER 2004
Dialogues
June

Kensington, London

Afternoon Talk

Nathan: To point effectively to our true nature, it is necessary to be clear with regard to the concepts that are used. I speak of Consciousness, oneness, wholeness, with its two simultaneous aspects of awareness and the content of awareness. The two aspects—awareness and content of awareness—are not separate: they are one. Awareness is the registering or cognising of all that presently appears as the content of awareness. Nothing else is ever going on apart from this registering of all that presently appears. The registering is the content—oneness. Within awareness, all appears as the content—every-thing appearing in no-thing. We can refer to the content of awareness as images—visual images, sounds, thoughts, sensations, emotions, etc.

Ordinarily, the awareness aspect of Consciousness, of oneness, is overlooked. The content of awareness, the arising images, appear to have a mesmerising quality, referred to traditionally as maya. One of the thought images that appears within the content is the primary or 'I' thought. This 'I' thought arises in conjunction with the body image, and is assumed to be an integral part of the character. When this 'I' is assumed then all other thoughts become 'my' thoughts, and the succession of arising thoughts (seen as 'my' thoughts) is what is referred to as the psychological self-sense or mind.

It may be helpful to see these thoughts as balloons arising with messages written on them, as in a cartoon comic. With the overlooking of the awareness aspect of our true nature and the focus on and mesmerisation with the content—in other words, identification as the character—the messages on the thought balloons appear as a story which seems real. So although the content actually arises presently in awareness, this mesmerisation with the thought story appears as a distraction 'from' or 'out of' presence, an extension into an imagined past and future—the story of this character. Memory and anticipation, past and future, are in fact simply thoughts arising presently.

When there is identification as a character, there is a sense of separation from everything else, from all apparent others, a sense of being located as a particular image. With this sense of separation, there is simultaneously an intuition of our true nature as oneness, and this disparity is what appears in the play of life as the motivation for the search for oneness. There is already only oneness or wholeness, and yet, when there is this mesmerising focus exclusively on the content aspect of oneness, there is a search *for* oneness. And this is the play of life: oneness in search of itself.

The analogy of a movie appearing on a screen is useful here. The movie is the content, the screen is awareness—together they are one. This screen is a multi-dimensional screen—the movie is appearing *in* the screen. Everything is appearing on this background of the multi-dimensional screen, so that within this movie, Consciousness—wholeness—oneness—is always perceiving itself as all forms.

Consciousness appears immanently as everything. Oneness is already Your true nature. 'You', oneness, are only ever seeing Yourself as all forms, but this fact is overlooked in the mesmerisation with the thought story. All forms of seeking—not just so-called 'spiritual seeking' or seeking oneness under the label of non-duality, but all forms of seeking—seeking for material satisfaction, for a comfortable place to live, for a fulfilling job—all of this is the search for oneness, for wholeness.

And so today, arising presently as the content of awareness, the present configuration of oneness, is a roomful of characters in search of their true nature. Oneness appears immanently as the room and every character, immersed in the thought story of seeking for itself, projecting so-called awakening as a future event. But—right now—there is already only one hundred percent awakeness; oneness appearing immanently in its two aspects of awareness and content of awareness, seemingly mesmerised by its own thought story.

Questioner: *I have a question. This must sound pretty insane but I don't see why wholeness should take itself off and go in search of itself. Why would it do that?*

There isn't a reason. The question arises from mesmerisation with the thought story.

But it just doesn't seem to make sense why wholeness becomes mesmerised and has to ask itself questions.

It doesn't have to ask itself questions, there's no necessity for any of it. It is simply the play of life arising in this way. It's all the cosmic entertainment.

In the thought story there is a search for meaning and a looking for a way out of it all—whereas when it's seen to be simply a story arising presently, an extension into past and future existing merely in thought, then the seriousness goes out of the quest for oneness. There is simply registering of the present content of awareness. This is all that is ever happening. This is already presence, already oneness.

There is mesmerisation, identification as the thought story, but there is no one who is mesmerised. The 'I' is only apparent, part of the happening. Everything is happening entirely spontaneously of its own accord. There is nothing that 'you' are doing. This message is not a prescription *for* oneness—it's a description *of* it.

You're just a tourist in the play.

No. 'You' are no specific thing. Your true nature is oneness—no-thing and every-thing. Oneness is the whole play.

So is it that all questions are oneness overlooking itself and jumping into identification?

34

There's no 'jumping into' identification. Identification is an appearance in the play, registering in awareness—the movie appearing on the screen.

So identification arises and then it's seen through.

Yes.

I very much like your analogy of a multi-dimensional screen. I had pictured a flat screen—as in the cinema—and so, until now, the analogy has never quite done it for me.

Yes, so this movie is playing on and *within* the screen. Another nice analogy that we can use is that all of this is the body of the one, and all the human characters are little cells circulating around in the body of the one. They are simply viewing points. Oneness is viewing itself via each of these cells, within and as itself.

❀   ❀   ❀

So there is this body-mind and a thought arises—for instance, 'I am hungry'—and the brain reacts to that thought.

No, it's simpler than that. There's no cause and effect. There is a play of images being presently registered. A body is appearing, simultaneously with a sensation of hunger, and also simultaneously with the thought, 'I am hungry'.

So what's doing the registering then?

No-thing is registering every-thing. This registering, or no-thing, is what the concept 'awareness' points to.

It can't be the 'I' thought because the 'I' thought, the person, doesn't exist anyway.

The 'I' thought is part of the content, part of what is being registered. No-thing is registering.

So are we trying to understand this with the mind?

There is no mind. The term 'mind' is used in a somewhat confusing way to represent the thoughts appearing and disappearing presently in awareness, and so seeming to constitute a stream of thoughts. This apparent stream of thoughts—when seen objectively as single images appearing and disappearing—is not problematic, but when labelled 'mind', it is presumed to constitute an actual entity. It is a phantom. No thought can understand anything. Thoughts are merely inert images—message balloons.

Where do they arise from?

It's a complete mystery, as is all of the arising content. They simply appear within awareness as part of the content.

The difficulty of course is that the mind shifts these thoughts together into a time sequence and so spins its own story, doesn't it? Is that how it is?

There is no mind. The mind *is* the succession of thoughts, so there *is* no mind as an entity that could do anything with thoughts or spin a story. The apparent succession of thoughts is already the story.

So the thoughts are doing the weaving—it's the other way around?

The thoughts aren't actually doing anything. They are merely images, arising in succession and so appearing to form a story.

And we don't know where the thoughts come from—it's a complete mystery.

Yes.

So we're on a hiding to nothing really! But who strings the thoughts together?

When the 'I' thought has been assumed, then the succession of arising thoughts appears to form a continuous solid entity called 'mind'. It's like a propeller: when it's still, it's seen as two or three blades, but when it's whirling around—the apparent succession of thoughts—then it appears as an entity.

The story.

Yes. This is what we're calling 'mind', but in fact mind has no existence—it's just an apparent succession of arising thoughts. The story formed in thought is no more real than a story formed by a succession of messages strung together to form a novel. There can be involvement in a novel, but only when it's picked up and read. It could just be left on the shelf.

Can you say also that there's actually no control over whether there is mesmerisation or not—it just happens?

That's right, yes.

And the apparent unfolding—you have no control over that either.

No, there is simply unfolding.

So to say that you're going to do something or not do something ...

That's the thought story. But it's not 'your' thought story—it's just the thought story presently appearing or happening.

So you just let it all happen.

'You' don't let it all happen—it's already happening. Maybe the 'I' will be undermined, maybe not.

This is all heard over and over and over, but it still occurs that doing takes place. And that feels wrong.

All of this is the thought story—maybe it appears within this play that it seems to need to be heard over and over again. That is the nature of these talks. There is simply this continual reminding of our true nature, that there is only already awakeness, oneness.

❋   ❋   ❋

Do you still have the sense of being a separate person?

There isn't necessarily any sudden dropping of the 'I', but maybe the 'I' is seen through. Perhaps there is more of the remembering of our true nature and less of a sense of being located 'inside' a body; more of a sense of the body simply arising here along with everything else, and appearing as a viewing or experiencing centre—like our cells in the 'body of the one' analogy. When the thought story running simultaneously with this bodily appearance is seen through, then ease is revealed, the tension goes out of it all.

So is there still sometimes a forgetting for the character Nathan, then?

If Nathan describes in a concrete way what is the life of the character here, then within the play it appears to promote continued mesmerisation with the thought story—perhaps comparing the life of Nathan with 'my' life ... Nathan maybe has something that 'I' don't, so therefore 'I' need to awaken, etc.

But Nathan is merely one image appearing amongst all the others. This is all the appearance of oneness, as these images, and it just happens that the Nathan image seems to have the function of appearing in the play to point this out.

But for the character Nathan there must have been a story of all this unfolding. Can you describe how that happened?

Well, when we focus on the character Nathan—that there was a point where the character Nathan realised something or changed in some way—then already there is involvement with the thought story, a projection into past. And this appears to support the thought story, the assumption of 'I', and the idea that 'I' will realise or recognise what Nathan has recognised 'in the future'. This is the way the thought story is supported within the play.

Whereas this little scene in the play appears to be about the undermining—the seeing through—of the story.

Presence is easily overlooked if Nathan starts harping on about some event, some point in time when there was realisation. All that encourages the mesmerisation with the thought story. In fact there is simply the registering of all that presently appears. Nothing else is happening.

❀   ❀   ❀

Everything is just happening?

Yes.

It's as insubstantial as a dream at night?

Yes, but with this daytime dream, there is no waking up out of the dream. What we are referring to as the recognition of our true nature as oneness is merely recognising it *is* a dream.

So Nathan at one stage was in a forgetting ...

No, no, there was never Nathan at a 'stage'—there is only the present appearance of Nathan.

'Nathan at a stage' is a story?

Yes, Nathan at some stage—'when something happened'—is a story, a story arising presently.

Nathan is a picture appearing now, and the history of Nathan is the thought story appearing now, just for entertainment in the dream?

Yes, all there is presently of Nathan is an image appearing at the front of the room.

What gymnastics we do with thought forms!

'We' don't do anything with thought forms.

Why can't we just remain in the maya *and enjoy the show?*

Yes, if there is identification as the character,

mesmerisation, and the character has a yacht in the bay and a few million in the bank, sunny days, happy families, the good life—then yes, mesmerisation is absolutely fine! (*laughter*)

But when you get really ill or something, then you go back to seeking.

There is seeking to get out of the play. All the while the play is going well, then all seems absolutely fine.

But what does it matter if one thinks like that anyway?

'One' isn't thinking like that—it's all happening as a story, as a play. But yes, there is no point to seeking and recognising. There is no more point or 'special-ness' to this scene in the play, with the story of seeking and recognising our true nature, than there is to any other scene of 'ordinary' life, or seeking for material happiness, etc.

So why are we trying to see then?

'We' aren't trying to see anything—this struggle to see is happening as a scene in the play.

Consciousness is a rotten old thing tormenting us with all these unhappy things happening to us. (laughter)

Right on! Let's all go and get drunk! (*laughter*)

East Sutton, Kent

One to One

Why are objects not the important thing but Consciousness itself is?

OK, we really need to clarify what we mean by Consciousness. Consciousness is wholeness, or oneness, which we can say has two aspects: awareness and the content of awareness. So what you are referring to as objects is the content of awareness—the images that are appearing and being registered in awareness. This idea that the content of awareness is unimportant is a misconception. It stems from the traditional idea of spirituality, which is to try to escape from the material—or the content, and that's why the material is often negated. But if there is only Consciousness—which is awareness and content of awareness—then the content is completely and equally as important as awareness.

But it can't exist on its own, the material.

Awareness and content of awareness are simultaneous—

they are one. But for the purpose of our conversation we may describe them as two *aspects* of Consciousness, of oneness.

So often one hears, 'All there is, is Consciousness,' and I'm grappling with that, thinking, 'Well, Consciousness is not a material thing—it's an awareness of the material.'

Consciousness—in the sense that we're using it here, Consciousness with a capital C—is wholeness or oneness, not consciousness as we would normally use the term.

As in 'I am conscious of this.'

That's right. So Consciousness is wholeness, oneness, and this oneness must include the material.

Yes.

So we have our two concepts: awareness and content of awareness. These are the two aspects or facets of Consciousness.

Right, right. So the oneness...

... is the registering of everything that is being registered. It's awareness of the content of awareness. And they arise simultaneously. They are inseparable. So there is no need to negate the arising objects. They are an aspect of the whole.

Right, so where does thought fit into this? I believe you speak of thought as part of the content.

Yes, arising as part of the content of awareness is thought, and because it has an ethereal-type nature it's kind of overlooked. In fact, what we need to do is to treat it as an image appearing within the content. Simultaneous with bodily appearance arises the 'I' thought.

The 'me' thought.

The 'me', yes, and because it seems to arise in conjunction with this body here and not that body over there, it is automatically assumed as an integral part of bodily life. It goes unquestioned. It's like putting an overcoat on and then forgetting that you've got the overcoat on.

The pseudo-subject.

That's right, when the 'I' thought arises, apparently in conjunction with this particular body, then the pseudo-subject appears but has no actuality. It's what we term the psychological self-sense. So this 'I' thought is like an overcoat, and then all other thoughts that arise become 'my' thoughts, from the point of view of this pseudo-subject.

So it becomes dual—subject-object.

Yes exactly, but in actuality there is no subject-object,

no duality. Remember, we are not using our concepts of awareness and content of awareness in a subject-object sense. They are inseparable as *aspects* of wholeness.

That's fantastic, that way of seeing that there is no subject-object.

Yes, the awareness is the no-thing, and the content of awareness is the every-thing. But with the arising of the 'I' thought—rather than no-thing and every-thing—we take ourselves to be 'something'.

Yeah, so when there is writing with this pen, there is this notion that 'I' am writing and this is a pen I'm writing with.

Yes.

It still creeps back, this subtle sense of separation of objects and things.

Yes.

Now in terms of the story, in terms of duality, of course, yes, we go along with that—otherwise I'd write on the carpet or write with my finger.

Yes, but with the intrinsic knowing that is our true nature, the play of life is simply seen through. So it appears as though separation is a fact, but it's seen through. It's seen for what it is.

A lot of other people I've listened to over the years have talked about the suddenness of this realisation, that it's not in time, although I've heard you say that it unfolds gradually.

There is only the present, but within the play of life there is the appearance of the gradual unfolding of the recognition of our true nature.

Yes, indeed, because as I've been reading this and reading that, the understanding and all the other concepts are dropping away ... So it appears to be in time, it appears to be a gradual thing. But the actual realisation itself—with reference to your cycle ride in the lanes in Clarity*—is a kind of sudden apperception or glimpse. Maybe it's more than a glimpse—maybe it's a sudden dropping away of everything, I don't know.*

It seems with many characters that there is a gradual unfolding of the recognition of their true nature as part of the story in the play of life—that is, first, understanding developing, and then eventually becoming obsolete as it dissolves into knowing.

Therefore what you speak of as 'actual realisation' may not necessarily be marked by any particular event or happening, or it may seem to be just a very small shift in perception—along the lines of, 'Well that's obvious—that's kind of been known all along.'

Yes, yes.

Now there can also be what you call a 'sudden

apperception', or glimpse, or dropping away of the 'me' but …

Really? A complete dropping away?

Yes, but that's not necessarily permanent. That's why I gave emphasis to the gardening and cycling event in *Clarity* specifically to illustrate this point. As that event arose, so did the idea, 'Ah, this is enlightenment, this is awakening!' As the event proceeded, a slight feeling of panic arose—that the event might cease—so there was a grasping to hold onto it as the sense of 'I' returned.

You mean the maya *returning as it were?*

Yes, the gradual return of the pseudo-subject.

Claiming that—claiming to be the doer of it.

Yes, exactly. So these kinds of events aren't necessarily helpful, in fact—because there is, generally, a returning of the 'I'. More rarely, there are characters where there is a sudden and continuous dropping, a 'permanent' dropping of the pseudo-self. Usually, though, there is a gradual recognition of oneness permeating into the play. It's not a recognition by the character, though—it's rather that the psychological self-sense is being seen through.

Being seen through by?

By no one. Consciousness is becoming aware of its true nature as no-thing—and also everything—over what appears as time in the play, in appearance as the character.

So can you just go through that again, that last phrase: becoming aware of its true nature as no-thing?

... and everything. So there is awareness and content of awareness, but without this middleman, the pseudo-subject, because the pseudo-subject is seen through. It's quite likely that this pseudo-subject still continues to arise, but it's now seen through. There is innate knowing, which is our true nature.

This knowing—it's not the witness that is often referred to?

No, the witness is where there is still a subject-object type of thing going on. In witnessing there is no longer exclusive identification with the content of awareness—instead there is residing *as* awareness, but without full recognition of—and resting as—one-ness. What we are speaking of as knowing is simple presence—resting as 'what is' in the recognition of our true nature.

So there is no knower but just knowing?

Yes, we *are* this knowing.

So if a bird sound is manifesting in Consciousness, as

Consciousness, then the hearing of it is, at the same time, actually the sound of it. They are one and the same thing.

Yes.

It's terribly simple in that sense.

It's so simple. It's so simple that it's nearly always overlooked. There's no need for the 'me' to disappear. There's actually no need to get into the technicalities of witnessing or knowing or anything else. There is *only* ever this knowing—oneness, always immediate, always right here.

We're looking for something huger, bigger. We're looking for this God-like kind of experience, for this amazing 'high'.

That's right. We're looking maybe for the more blissful aspect to all of this—the 'enhanced' version of it, the ecstasy—which *can* happen but which isn't necessary.

It can happen because it's happened to composers, musicians, whatever—or to people listening to their music and so on and so forth.

But it's not necessary for wholeness. Wholeness is already the case, right now. There hasn't even got to be a *feeling* of wholeness or oneness.

That can arise, can't it?

Yes, it can arise suddenly as a transcendental-type

event. But also, as the recognition of our true nature unfolds, there is less of a feeling of being located as the body or as something 'inside the body'. There is just a body appearing, thoughts appearing, trees and hills appearing and all the rest of it.

So, the revealing of our true nature arises as a story in the play—this searching for what I truly am.

Yes. When the 'I' thought arises and is assumed, then there is a kind of inherent tension in that. It's like a coiled spring, keeping the whole thing going—the search to become whole in all its forms.

Yes, it does feel like that tremendously. Is there a sense then that there is—I'm just echoing words that I've heard—a releasing of that 'I', but no one who can release it?

That's right.

There is no one who can release that coiled spring.

There is simply the releasing, a gradual unfolding in the play. Ease begins to arise, or rather be revealed. The 'I' will be seen through at times and at others it won't. Gradually there is a settling where the 'I' is naturally seen through.

Does it just naturally wither away?

It's seen through, seen for what it is, and so it doesn't have its mesmerising quality any more.

It would be nice to have that happen suddenly.

Exactly. That's what the whole seeking for oneness game is about, because we hear of these cases where it's happened suddenly—but in fact, when we look at it, they are fairly rare.

But at what point is the ultimate understanding or realisation there? Because of this seemingly gradual unfolding, it seems there's got to be a moment where you say, 'Oh yeah, that's it.'

I think it would be good here if we looked at the term 'understanding' and see that understanding is part of the play, and in actuality nothing ever needs to be understood. So there is no 'ultimate understanding'. Within the play, understanding arises in relation to *seeking* our true nature, but there is no understanding *of* it. What initially arises as understanding is actually the percolating into the play of knowing. From the point of view of oneness, there is never any need for understanding. Understanding only appears as part of the play and, with the relaxing into knowing, understanding becomes obsolete. There is no 'ultimate knowing', but as there is more of a resting in knowing and the 'I' is seen for what it is, then cares about 'ultimate' conditions will subside anyway. It's from the viewpoint of the assumed 'I' that seeking for 'ultimate' or anything else takes place.

That's good, that's interesting. I think I see what is meant by suddenness.

Yes, it's sudden because the recognition of your true nature is always presently—*but* it's not necessarily continuous. It's initially sporadic. Sometimes the 'I' is seen through and sometimes not.

Right, right.

This is a play about Consciousness coming to know its own true nature as already whole, already one, via the medium of the play.

Yeah.

Seeking and understanding become obsolete.

Hmm ... yes, it seems to be that way. There seems to be less and less seeking, although I have to say that I'm enjoying this—going through this. There is a sense of 'Oh yes, yes!', a sense of recognition. I was just wondering—if I had never come across these concepts and I'd gone on in life in my own sort of way, just kind of enjoying concepts and building up all this sort of stuff ... Well, I'm talking conceptually now.

Yes, if the play isn't seen for what it is, then hypothesising is a distraction from presence, from 'what is'. Much of seeking involves hypothesising, looking at thoughts and ideas from the point of view of 'I'. Meanwhile, the 'I'—which is only another thought—goes uninspected.

A lot of assumptions are made outside of immediate perception. So, for instance, I could have a blazing row with you now about America or Iraq, and of course all we are talking about ...

... is completely conceptual. All that presently is, is a room with two characters appearing in it.

This is what appears to me increasingly, how bizarre all this is.

Yes.

And this is very peculiar for me, because I'm feeling that the old life—being involved in these kinds of arguments and ideas and all that sort of thing—is becoming increasingly ... thin.

It's seen through, yes.

It's a very odd feeling, isn't it?

It can be, yes.

And even though you seem to know it, there's a strong feeling that needs to be worked through, that the story needs a reconciliation, or that it needs a kind of solving of what is thought to be a particular problem. It all seems to be in time and so on and so forth. And there may even be an awareness that this is ... Do you find that yourself, that feelings still arise?

Absolutely, yes, of course. Everything arises in the

same way, but it's seen through. When the 'I' is seen for what it is, then thoughts, feelings, whatever, are just images, events, happenings. Appropriate responses arise but 'I' am no longer striving to make it all work, because 'I' is only a thought. Everything is spontaneously arising in awareness—as the content of awareness—and the 'I' has only ever been an 'addition' to all the rest of it. The 'I' may still arise but there's no need for it to disappear. It's only a play, after all.

Is that the only kind of ingredient in the whole thing, that's creating all this stress?

The 'I' is not creating anything because it is only a thought, an image, but *within the play* there is tension associated with the assumption of 'I'.

So all that one can do—all that can happen—is the seeing through of that.

Yes. But 'one' can't do anything about it at all. Because the 'one' that would see through it—the 'I' that would see through it—is the very 'I' itself. So all that we can say is that this play runs its course and that this 'I' is gradually seen through.

It's seen through by no one.

It's seen through by no one.

There's nothing much to ask after all that, is there?

It's very simple. It really is. And that's why, in this little scene of seeking in the play, if these questions are not being answered in a way that supports the 'I', that supports the psychological self-sense, but in a way that instead undermines it, then the questions arise less and less. It is noticed that as thoughts arise, they are adopted as 'my' thoughts, from the point of view of this pseudo-subject, and are voiced as questions. These thoughts may still continue to arise, but when the 'I' is seen through, and the seeking winds down, then the questions fall naturally away. Thoughts are just part of the scenery.

They pass by.

When the seeking and questioning die down, then all of this—even what we have talked about today—becomes obsolete. There is everything presently as it is, without any explanation for any of it.

Without any explanation ... without any comment on it.

No, no comment is needed.

Or any need to understand it or any need to clarify it or assess what it is.

No.

I'm glad to hear that. (laughter) *Thanks a lot. I enjoyed that, thank you very much.*

East Sutton, Kent
One-Day Retreat

Nathan, all the stuff about awakening seems to become an irrelevance, more and more, and there's more a being puzzled about, 'What's this all about?' It seems to become so irrelevant. I don't know how to explain it properly.

Well, there isn't a point to it. This movie—this play of life—appears, and when the thoughts are seen for what they are and there is no longer the play of identification as the character, then it is noticed that there is already awakeness and everything is arising spontaneously. Everything is on 'auto-pilot', so there is a play today of there being a roomful of characters, questions being asked and answering going on, but nobody's at the helm.

I think the auto-pilot image is very clear.

Yes. If we use the analogy of a movie appearing on a screen, there's nothing there but images appearing—the screen and the movie go together. The images appear on the screen and that's it. It's only when there is this mesmerisation in thought that there is the idea appearing that something can be done about it, that there's a point to it all. But that's just the play.

Aren't these images solid? They're three-dimensional.

Yes, it's a multi-dimensional movie, being viewed from within the movie, not being viewed by a viewer from outside. This *is* the movie. Using an analogy of the human characters representing cells within the 'body' of Consciousness—viewing points, then we can see that this movie is being viewed from all these different points within itself by Consciousness. Consciousness *is* the movie, and is viewing and experiencing itself as each character.

There was a Woody Allen film some years ago where a character does actually step out of the movie—I've forgotten which film it was, but maybe we as seekers are trying to do that.

Yes, but there is nothing outside of the movie. There is only the movie and the present registering of it from 'within' the movie. The registering and this that is being registered—which is wholeness, Consciousness.

And no need to escape.

No, that's the goal of traditional spirituality: escape from identification as the content into the awareness aspect.

But that's not it either.

No, our true nature is wholeness with the simultaneous aspects of awareness *and* the content of awareness.

Knowing is deepening here, but there is often still a sense of separation.

It is unlikely initially that there will be a felt sense of oneness. But as there is more of a resting in knowing, then this sense of being bodily confined may seem to dissipate, so that there is still a body appearing here but it's not 'my' body any more. There may be less of a concrete feeling of being 'I—this body'.

And the apparent evolving can be so subtle it's hardly noticed.

Yes. This is the play—of seeking, of coming to talks, of reading books, so that this exclusive identification as the character has already been fairly well undermined in the case of most of the characters in the room.

But 'out there in the world', this message with regard to our true nature isn't commonly propagated. It's not permeating into the play as part of 'everyday life'. So, within the play, there is a constant tendency of forgetting of our true nature. All the characters are behaving as individual characters, completely unaware that our identity is the same. When there is reminding of your true nature, it's not hard to see that everything, every form, is Yourself. There is still, however, the *appearance* of separation, distance, perspective, as a functional aspect of the play.

❋   ❋   ❋

It seemed as though I chose to come here today, but at the same time I kind of know it just happened.

Everything is just happening—the movie on the screen, including the thought story. So it seems as though there is an 'I' that's choosing to come here today, but there is simply this automatic happening of arriving here today and the thought story running automatically. No one's thinking thoughts—they are simply arising in awareness. Everything is being registered presently: the content of awareness being registered in awareness. When there is focus on the thought story, it appears as if there is the making of choices and decisions and all the rest of it, whereas in fact it's all completely spontaneous—every-thing presently arising in no-thing.

So there's no choosing?

There is apparent choosing in the play. If someone says, 'Do you want a cup of tea?' and you say 'Yes' ... If we could just switch the movie soundtrack off for a minute, there's someone standing there, and the next minute there's a cup of tea arriving and then the drinking of it. It's just that the soundtrack—including the thoughts about choosing, etc—is added in.

Everything is running on autopilot, but there is the appearance of choosing, which spices up the entertainment.

With simple presence, all this concern over choice becomes obsolete. When there is identification as the character, then all of this philosophising is a 'distraction' from presence. Thoughts about choosing are arising and there is distraction in them. Anything that arises within the content—a discussion about choice, thoughts about choice or anything else—is the entertainment of the play. And when there is recognition of this being a play, then the desire no longer appears for any of it to change at all. There is presently what is.

Just being.

Yes, without concern for any of this. While there is still this in and out of identification as the character, then this kind of a talk is appropriate, but when all of this begins to die—this whole seeking drama—and there is more of the 'remembering' of our true nature as oneness, then there is simply present living.

Amongst other apparent characters.

Yes. There is no longer involvement with all the hypothesising and concern as to whether there's choosing or all the rest of it. An ordinary life is lived in this innate knowing. So it's not that there's necessarily bliss, but there is an ease with it all. The seeking dies. That agitation that is the seeking dies.

Then what's the point of living?

There isn't one. This movie of life is the cosmic entertainment. That question stems from the viewpoint of 'me', the identified character in the movie. When there is identification as the character, then there is the constant looking for a reason for it, looking for a point. And it seems that the 'ultimate' point of living is what is commonly referred to as 'awakening'— re-awakening into oneness.

But oneness is already the case. There is already one hundred percent awakeness, and when the thought story is no longer taken seriously, then there is presently what is. There's nothing outside of the present. There's no past or future life of this character. The story may still remain but it's no longer taken seriously.

Is it true to say then that thoughts are only ever about past and future?

Thoughts can be *about* the present.

When it's to do with the present, we're actually experiencing it, rather than thinking about it.

The thought story may or may not be appearing simultaneously with other images, and the thoughts may be about the images, rather than a distraction from them. All thought is arising presently, and the nature of many of these thoughts is to distract from presence. Some of these thoughts *about* the present are what is referred to as understanding, which is the reflection of *knowing* arising in thought form. We're reminded of our true nature in thought form, but because thoughts (as part of the content of awareness) are fleeting, (they're always passing through), when a reminder arises—which we refer to as understanding—it can be 'forgotten' again, it can disappear. Whereas when thoughts are seen for what they are, then there is an innate knowing *as* our true nature, which requires no thought. And understanding is obsolete.

What's really strange is that sometimes there's very much just being in that space without thought and even knowing that this is what it is, this is presence. And yet there is still this very subtle expectation that there needs to be something else.

Yes, but that is still the mesmerisation, even if, as you say, subtly: the idea that oneness can be found within the content of awareness, or in escape from it. When there is reminding of our true nature or there is innate knowing, then that immediately cuts through the seeking within the content or the motive to escape. Our true nature is oneness—not exclusively the content or exclusively awareness—but there can be the play of moving in and out of identification as the character, however subtly.

There can often be a recognition of our nature as oneness, and yet there is still a very subtle waiting game going on, waiting for *the* final event, *the* final happening ... Whereas as knowing permeates into the play, ease is revealed as seeking drops away, and that subtle waiting is undermined more and more.

So it absolutely can seem like an unfolding.

Sure. Consciousness has infinite possibilities going here. The traditional idea that it is limited to the 'final event' game is a bit old hat now. There is only presently what is, so whatever is happening—including any seeming unfolding—is already it.

❀   ❀   ❀

I hear often that the silence is in the gaps, and that God or presence or whatever you call it is in the gaps, and to listen to the silence between the words. And so, in a way, that's what happens—if the silence becomes louder than the words, then you just sort of let it go and just be with that silence. It's very powerful.

Sure, yes, but Consciousness is not only the gaps. There is only Consciousness. Sometimes the play takes the form of quite an intensive conversation— sometimes there are quiet spaces, there are gaps.

Do you really need to keep hearing reminders necessarily?

No.

Once you've heard the message a few times, theoretically you could …

Absolutely so—but for as long as you tend to show up at these meetings, then the reminding happens.

You say, 'Awareness and content'—this is a brief formula you can use to remind yourself?

No, 'you' can't. But reminding in this way may arise as a happening in the play.

❋　　　❋　　　❋

I sometimes think that there's not very much of life so I'd better get on—crack on and do all the things that my sad little mind has decided that I should be going for. And in the process missing all the beauty around us.

Most often that's what this play of life is: Consciousness appearing as a 'someone' constantly trying to get somewhere.

To get it done.

Sure, yeah, to get it done, so that there can be a resting at the *end* of it—rather than *in* it, *as* it, presently.

It's relentless, isn't it?

From the point of view of the identified character, yes. This search for the end of problems is never-ending, because there will always be a new problem.

What is so amusing about this is that—if it's true (as I'm starting to see it is) that every moment is the invitation to see it—whilst you're breaking your neck, running around bursting your bottles, doing this, that and the next thing, every single moment there's something saying, 'Stop! Look!'

Sure, amidst all the rushing around this message creeps in. It is the permeating into the play of the reminding of our true nature.

I can remember being exhausted by seeking but still not getting it. Just being absolutely tired and fed up and, I suppose, kind of depressed. Because you realise it's all pointless but you still haven't seen clearly through the story. You're still waiting for some kind of awakening.

It's always being projected into the future, even subtly as a waiting game.

It's not that bliss is what I'm really talking about appearing ... But having said that, that ease of life, that sense of allowing the beauty of everything that's going on about you into your life—embracing it, if you like—it hasn't been there. It hasn't been happening for me for many years. I suppose that's all part of the game, really. At some deep level, I still believe that unless I'm achieving something, unless I'm doing my thing—as everyone else seems to be doing their thing—I'm somehow failing.

As the identified character, we appear to be doing, because the ideas arise in conjunction with the actions. The story is that 'I am doing this', whereas in fact the pictures are appearing on the screen and the thought story runs alongside.

I've just noticed what I did there: I divided myself off by saying 'I' or 'my' experience. But that's only within the game—we appear to be doing that.

Yes. When the seeking game drops, though, there's no longer any concern about using the terms 'I', 'me', 'my', because they no longer have this reference to the identified character.

The personal.

Yes.

❀   ❀   ❀

So when the 'I' is seen through, seeking stops and there is peace.

An ease arises. It's seen that there has actually only ever been this ease, but that the agitation of seeking is a focus that obscures the ease. So that when there is less of a focus on the play of being exclusively identified as the character, then the ease—which is underlying the agitation—comes to the fore. The agitation dissipates.

So, in fact, it isn't ordinary for you?

It is only from the point of view of the seeking character that the ease is anticipated as extraordinary. In fact, seeking seems more extraordinary!

So the extraordinary becomes ordinary.

Yes, in the sense of it being simply natural and easeful. Extraordinary from the viewpoint of the seeker, but natural and ordinary when seeking drops.

The ordinary becomes entirely satisfying, in a way?

Yes, nothing extraordinary is required.

It feels sometimes, though, that what keeps the identification going is, for instance, issues about how I bring up my daughter. How I try to exercise some sort of control over her life. I know intrinsically there's no one there and nothing really matters, but I still seem to be determined to have a fight with her every night, that she will do her homework! And this gets really, really deep into 'me' and 'her' and big desires—and falling completely into the idea that there's a 'me' that can do anything.

Yes, of course. If it were just a question of straightforward thought, then it would be all cut and dried really, wouldn't it? However, in this play of life, thought often appears in conjunction with feeling and unless (as with thought) it is seen objectively, as part of the scenery in the play, then it seems to give the thoughts a 'charge'. The mesmerisation with the thought story is even more compelling.

Yes, yes. That's very helpful actually, because thoughts coming and going can be seen through, but if they are not separated from the feeling content, then they do indeed seem very compelling.

This is the nature of the play: that at first there is complete involvement as the character, then there is a seeing of the play for what it is, and this ease of being is revealed—everything is simply as it is. So then the arguing with the daughter about the homework is no longer a dilemma. It's just something that happens presently.

❀   ❀   ❀

I suppose you hear these terms like 'living in chaos' and 'living on the razor's edge' and it all sounds quite exciting—to be on the razor's edge.

Yeah, exactly. It's thrilling, isn't it? When you're getting onto the path of 'spiritual' seeking—to be on the razor's edge! To be told, 'It's just the ordinary,' the reaction would be, 'Oh no, I don't want to hear that!' As we said earlier, though, what we're calling here 'the ordinary' would be seen—from the 'razor's edge' point of view—as the extraordinary. The ease that is revealed in the absence of seeking—if it were experienced immediately, without the story of the gradual breaking down of exclusive identification as the character within the play—would seem like the absolutely extraordinary.

The paradox of seeking is that we're seeking for what we already are—as you say, wholeness or oneness—but rather than as what already is, we're seeking for God as some big intelligence behind the scenes.

Yes, but there's no intelligence behind the scenes. *This is God. This* is what we traditionally term God. This is the immanent appearance of God, oneness, Consciousness, presence—as this roomful of characters. This is it. And as the search for wholeness subsides and ease is revealed, then seeking for God or oneness or enlightenment becomes ludicrous. There is no need—everything is as it is, it's OK already.

When you say the word 'search', it could just be anything— say there's anxiety and you don't want it to be there.

Yes, seeking takes many forms. We're talking in the context of these meetings about the search for awakening or so-called enlightenment, whereas it can be the search for being able to play the best game of football or for a new car or, as you say, to get over a feeling of anxiety or whatever. Consciousness is appearing as every character and has a different story of seeking running in each case.

In the case of the seeker who comes to talks of this nature the assumption may arise that this is a 'special' sort of search, and although it *is* an ultimate form of seeking—when our true nature is revealed then *all* seeking is seen through—it's not special. The identified character in the play is seeking for wholeness in whatever form it may take, and the seeing through of that identification—seeing it for what it is—is the end of the story of separation and seeking.

❀ ❀ ❀

Can you talk about why some people are able to transmit shakti?

In the play of life, *shakti* is a form of energy which the spiritual seeker sees as being significant for transformation and purification. It is the function of certain characters in the play to appear as being a channel for this energy via touch, gaze, etc.

Shakti transmission is a compelling part of the play, producing changes in state and perception. Often there is a suspension of identification as the character, in conjunction with what we might term transcendental experiencing and including also maybe psychic vision, the hearing of 'inner' sounds and spontaneous bodily movements. This is attributed to the awakening or movement of *kundalini*. In some characters, there is a tendency for the *kundalini* energy to move spontaneously without any form of transmission, and in others its movement is induced by certain psychotropic plants and drugs—mushrooms, cacti, LSD, etc. All of this is part of the entertainment of the play.

Someone was just talking to me about the 'no one's here' club, saying that that has sort of a dead feeling, that there has to be a perceptible feeling of energy.

The play of Consciousness appears differently as every character. In some cases there's seeking for the whole energy display and drama—whereas for others, simply in being reminded by a talk like today's there's an immediate recognition of our true nature, without any need for the fireworks.

So these people transmitting shakti—*do they try to create it?*

No, no, there's no internal character or 'I'—only the sense of one. Being a chooser or a doer in any way is entirely illusory. It's a play, a story arising in thought. It's all arising entirely spontaneously. Perhaps we can liken it to a dream at night which just appears out of nowhere.

In this play of life there are characters appearing where there may still be identification as the character, with the *apparent* ability to manipulate energy. From the point of view of that character, there is still the idea 'I am transmitting this energy'—rather than all of this being seen as a happening in the play.

So does that mean for someone who has this ability but yet in whom there still seems to be a lot of 'me' there—does that necessarily mean that liberation has not occurred?

Well, there is no liberation apart from present awakeness and this play of appearances. This present conversation—which is entirely hypothetical—is arising as an interesting diversion or distraction from presence. There can be involvement in all sorts of conversations about such stuff, and when there is the innate knowing of our true nature, all of this is interesting and fun. When there is still the tendency for mesmerisation with the arising thoughts, though, then all of this becomes serious stuff again. Thoughts arise such as, 'Oh, is he really enlightened or not? Is he liberated? Hmm, not quite sure about that!' And the thoughts are taken seriously. Do you see what I mean?

Oh yeah.

Liberation is assigned to another character 'out there'. 'That character is liberated ... Oh, *I* can't be liberated! ... Look at the stuff that they're able to do! ... Wow, all the enlightened talk they're coming out with!' So again, it's a part of the forgetting. Presence is overlooked in the involvement with the story. And in the story there are all sorts of colourful characters who appear to be 'enlightened', or possibly not. This is all the drama of the play.

On the same theme, let's say there's spiritual experience—hovering on the thirty-second level of heaven, bliss or whatever—and let's say that that's no more meaningful than having a cup of tea. But then also within the appearance there can be the complete disappearance of the self.

Of the psychological self-sense, you mean? Of the 'I'?

Yes, the total loss of this contraction into the self. And it could last for a few seconds or weeks or months, or it could be continuous. There seems to be a paradox, with this complete disappearance of the self, that on the one hand it has no significance whatsoever—while on the other hand, it's supremely significant, the expansion of the sense of self into everything.

Consciousness is already all that is. Therefore there is no expansion of the sense of self into everything. 'Expansion' is already the case, and there is only the *appearance* of contraction as the 'I'. There is simply the seeing through of the 'I' or self—so that it doesn't actually matter whether there is the appearance of 'I' or not, whether the psychological self-sense drops or not.

Now, for the seeker, it seems to matter tremendously because of the involvement with this whole drama. In this play, Consciousness is appearing as every character, and for every character there's a different storyline. So in some of the apparent characters, there may be a complete and continuous dropping of the psychological self-sense. In others, there is complete identification as the 'I'.

But there doesn't have to be any complete disappearance of this 'I' because what we're talking about here is the *seeing through* of the 'I'—the seeing of the 'I' for what it is, rather than waiting around for its complete disappearance. In this seeing through of the 'I' then, there is resting as our true nature.

If Nathan starts on now about there being the complete absence of 'I' here and 'Oh, it's beautiful and wonderful' and all the rest of it, then instead of there being this scene in the play now of the characters resting comfortably with things just as they are—with the 'I' being seen through—it appears to promote this whole search for the disappearance of the 'I'. If I start saying, 'The 'I' has completely disappeared here' and all the rest of it, then it's like dangling this golden carrot of so-called enlightenment or awakening.

What is being expressed here today is that there is *only* awakeness. There is only ever awakeness, but within awakeness, there is this mesmerisation as 'I'. When it is simply recognised that 'I' is just another thought, it's not required that 'I' completely or permanently disappears, and it's perfectly OK for this 'I' to come and go. It doesn't matter any longer. There's no longer seeking for the marvellous or for blissfulness because all is already OK. The ease that is revealed in seeing through the 'I' is enough.

❀　　❀　　❀

When there is a permanent residing in this, is there a deeper understanding as time passes?

Understanding doesn't deepen—understanding becomes obsolete. Understanding is only from the point of view of the identification as the character. When this knowing of your true nature begins to permeate into the play, initially it appears as seeking and understanding. But as this goes on, and intrinsic knowing permeates the play, then understanding becomes unnecessary.

Just part of the story.

Yes. You see, from the point of view of the character

in the play, understanding is everything. It seems that there is stuff to 'get'. But in fact that is just the permeating into the play of the recognition of your true nature via understanding. As knowing is revealed, then understanding is unnecessary, and it's seen that there's never any need for understanding, that at any moment there can be complete dropping of the psychological self-sense, and that none of this actually matters anyway. So there is no need for understanding. Understanding is the play.

When there is the present recognition of your true nature as oneness—simple presence—then what understanding is needed for that? There is presence—everything as it is: characters appearing, stories going on, earthquakes happening and tragedies, great joy, and all the rest of it. It's the play. Within the play, when there is identification as the character, all sorts of things can seem important but nothing actually is important. It's only important from the point of view of the play itself.

So say some things you've been interested in—anything, but mainly mind things, like philosophy and stuff—all of that would just drop?

Anything that's about the working out of this life as the character becomes obsolete. There's life as it is, and trying to work it out in any way is the seeking by the identified character. There's nothing to be worked out. There's simply the movie appearing on the screen.

In a practical way, though, if we talk of hobbies—like needlework or gardening or archaeology or something like that—then that will likely continue; the character has certain tendencies. But these things aren't about trying to find some way out of the play—they're about entertainment within the play. All of the stuff about trying to escape from the play, though, and trying to make it work becomes obsolete. There is a loss of interest in it.

But the play is still all there, because it cannot be otherwise—everything co-exists.

Of course.

And the play is still there.

Yes, a story may even still be running—but it's seen through, the mesmerisation is seen through. There is still the life of this character appearing, but the motive to escape from it is gone. It's seen for what it is. There's already oneness whether or not there is a story running within it. The story can still run but the story is known to be a story, and so an ordinary life appears.

Yet to the identified character in the play, this 'ordinary life' would seem extraordinary. This absence of existential tension or agitation would seem extraordinary.

If there's a sudden dropping of the psychological self-sense, then there might well be a release in the form of bliss or whatever. In what now appears as the ordinary, though, there's no longer the motive to seek bliss or anything else—it's seen through. It's all just part of the play. There is an ease that doesn't require any seeking.

Is that ease partly a recognition that there's nothing to be done and nothing that can be done?

All is already OK as it is. The 'I' that would do something is seen through. As the search to do something, to try to change it in any way, falls away, then ease or peace is not manufactured or created—it's what is already the case anyway and is simply obscured by the mesmerisation.

❀   ❀   ❀

The relaxing into ease seems to bring a spontaneity without too much thinking 'Can I do this or should I do this?' There is just the natural movement of whatever happens—including things which, certainly in my case, I would have never dreamed of doing, because I would have thought 'No, I can't do this—there are too many people—I can't speak in public!' or something like that. There are things that happen now where it's just walked into naturally, without this 'me' saying 'I can't do it.'

Yes. This 'me' saying 'I can't do it' is the story that's running alongside what's actually happening. And when we see through the thought story, the story may continue to arise but it's no longer believed, and so everything appears more spontaneous.

Sometimes you realise you are totally at ease with some-thing and there's a thought, 'This would not have hap-pened before.' It's not necessarily there all the time—it's just glimpsed now and then.

Yes, sure.

Because there is less baggage here about someone who is responsible for the world or for the character. I find it immensely helpful to think in terms of there being no doer—'I'm not creating my life, I'm not controlling things'—because it relieves me of a lot of the sense of guilt that I have to do something to change something. Apart from this narrow area I spoke of earlier with my daughter, where it's really sticky because of the emotional charge, the rest is becoming easier.

Yes, sure. From the point of view of the identified character in the play of life, these concepts of not being the doer and similar ones are very useful when they permeate into the play, because there is a kind of release of this whole baggage. So even when there is this unfolding in understanding still as the character, these concepts have a great capacity for release or relaxation *within the play.* But understand-ing never leads to any awakening from the identifica-tion as the character, because understanding is part of the play and simply becomes obsolete as knowing arises.

So when you're in the company of people who are deeply immersed in the play or deeply in their dreams and they're not conscious or aware of what we're talking about here, do you find yourself tempted to reveal any of this?

Not in the slightest, no.

Do you think that would be a pretty dangerous thing to do?

I don't know if it would be dangerous, but it would probably seem that we were speaking a load of mumbo-jumbo, wouldn't it? Any movement to explain to 'others' requires an investment in the story of a character here, and when that is seen through, stuff like that is no longer important. It's perfectly fine for all apparent others to be immersed in the play. Consciousness appears and is already awake as every character, but without the recognition. So when recognition arises, there's no need or agenda here to do anything about it.

Maybe if mesmerisation is dropping in a big way, the thought may arise, 'Wow this is revolutionary! This is absolutely amazing! I must tell everybody about this!' But hardly any of the characters are interested. Why should they be? Consciousness is already awake as every character and has no investment or special interest in the recognition of itself as Consciousness. In these talks a question is asked and a reply happens, but it's no more important than ordinary conversation within the play.

So does that mean that you find those kinds of exchanges equally entertaining?

Of course. If you go to a barbecue, all the talk there will usually be about material stuff and social chit-chat, so you join in. In the play, when you're the serious seeker on the path, on 'the razor's edge' of it, then small talk is taboo. You can't read novels—only the latest 'spiritual' book will do! When that trip falls away, though, whatever arises is fine. As the 'I' is seen through, all of the precious seeking drama dies a natural death.

There's not so much of a motive to come to the talks anymore but I seem to turn up anyway, just to hang out.

Well, think of it in terms of going to a club where you're discovering how to play pool. It's not that when you've sussed out the game you stop going—you still go there to hang out a bit—you know, have a beer and shoot a couple of frames.

That's a nice way of putting it. So where's the beer?

We drank it all at lunchtime. (*laughter*)
Well, I guess that's about it for today.

Thank you, Nathan.

Thank you for all the excellent questions.

A Phone Call with the Lady
from The North

To notice that there is awareness, with the content in it, isn't something that I can do, is it?

No. Noticing is a happening in the unfolding of the play of life whereby oneness—our true nature—is recognised via the medium of the play. Mesmerisation with content is seen through. There is a recognition of the awareness as being simultaneous with the content, the two aspects of oneness.

Yes, because there couldn't be the content if there wasn't awareness. The wall wouldn't be there if there wasn't awareness of the wall.

Yes, but more importantly, they arise simultaneously, they are simply two aspects of the one—of oneness, of wholeness. The wall is actually seeing itself!

Right, right. Now, previously you've lived in the world seeing it the way I do, right?

Well, 'we' are appearances of oneness. Nothing is seen differently here, but the thought story is seen through. Mesmerisation with the content aspect of oneness is no longer the exclusive theme. The very same viewing of all that appears happens, but the thought story is part of the landscape rather than a 'filter'—as it appears to be when there is identification as the 'I'.

Like seeming that you're the person, separate, looking at the wall.

Yes.

You've had that experience?

That is still *seemingly* the case now. That sense of separation—of a person looking at a wall—is functional. It's functional within the play, as part of the play. Without seeming distance and separation, the play wouldn't work.

Right. So there's nothing wrong with feeling that you're looking at a wall?

No, absolutely not!

So that doesn't have to change for recognising that oneness is what you really are.

Although there is still appearance as this character, there's the recognition that that isn't all we are. We are not *only* the person but also this registering *of* the person—awareness and also the content of awareness. Oneness is the whole thing—including the seeming separation. It's not as though anything has to change—there is already awareness right now, presently viewing the content.

Right, but not aware that it's awareness.

Well, within the play, the 'point' of this conversation appears to be about the constant reminding of our true nature, oneness in its two aspects of awareness and the content of awareness. There is registering and there is what is being registered.

That 'me' wants to do something, though!   (laughter)

What does the 'me' want to do then?

It wants to recognise something.

So, is the idea arising of 'objectivising' the awareness? To concretise it, to actually find it in amongst the content?

Yes, to know what it is.

Yes, but in fact it can't be known. It *is* the knowing, it is the registering of all that appears. It is no-thing registering every-thing.

Right.

There is seeking for some kind of ultimate knower—whereas, in fact, all there is is knowing. It's always immediate, always right now. If it is projected as an awakening that's going to happen in the future, then something is being overlooked.

I understand that there's never going to be any other time.

Right, so there must be *something* about the present that's being overlooked. These concepts of awareness and content of awareness are present pointers. We don't have to look to a future for them to arise.

No, no. So the 'me' thought coming up is all right—as you say, it's part of the landscape. But it gets overlooked and the story seems real.

Exactly.

The 'me' thought isn't the problem—it's when it's overlooked.

Yes.

But you've got no control over anything—it's just happening, isn't it?

Yes, so all that's going on here is a description, not a prescription.

But as a 'me' it feels that you do have an effect on what's happening.

That's right, yes.

And then a thought comes up, 'Well I don't have any effect—it's all just happening.' Because there can't be an effect if there isn't another time when there was a cause and there's only what's happening now.

Yes. This is what we refer to in the play as understanding—the reflection of knowing. There is still an 'I' understanding, but it often appears in the play to have a relieving effect.

So if I'm aware of that, then I've lost any feeling that I can make any kind of difference to anything that's going to happen.

Yes.

It's not very nice, in a way, to think that you don't have any effect on anything.

Yes, but now we're back in the story—whereas in actuality this 'me' that wants to have the effect is just a part of the present happening.

So it becomes something that you notice instead of trying to understand.

Yes, but 'you' don't notice it—there is simply noticing.

How do you step into recognising that that's what you are and you're not the 'me'? Ah! The 'me' thought can't do that—I suppose it's been trying to ...

Yes, the 'me' can't do it because the 'me' is what is seen through. All that can be said is that within the play of life, the mesmerisation with the thought story is gradually—or suddenly—seen through.

So in the play I've been a 'me' trying to see through it?

The 'me' trying to see through it is actually part of the story; it's the mesmerisation itself. That's all we're describing here: the end—or seeing through of—this mesmerisation.

Right. And don't go looking for it.

Well, it's not as though there's any choice in it. The play is on automatic pilot, it's all happening automatically: apparent identification as the character, involvement with the seeking—and then maybe the permeation into the play of the recognition of oneness.

So if I'm assuming that I'm the 'I', I can hear that there is oneness and that's my true nature, but I can't do anything about recognising that?

No, because the 'I' that's been assumed, the exclusive focus on the content aspect of oneness, is what is seen through or seen for what it is. The recognition permeates into the play, but it's not the 'I' that recognises it.

So it percolates in without me having to make any kind of struggle to try to understand it, because that's just furthering the thought that I'm an 'I' who can do something.

Yes, in the play it appears to reinforce the 'I'. Of course there could still be an apparent struggle.

I've got the first entrancement going on that I am the 'I' but I needn't add to it, or it needn't be added to.

That's right.

Right. So if anything happens that seems to lessen that, it will happen—but not by 'me' doing anything about it.

That's right. But within the play it may still appear that there is a 'me' doing something about it.

All the other thoughts seem easier to see objectively—it's the 'I' that seems to be separate and solid. It seems to be the one that sticks.

For years I've focused on all the instantaneous enlightenment stuff, that there's something going to click and that's going to be it. I know you say that it can be seen through immediately, but when you say that it can also percolate gradually, it allows me to relax. It seems that if it's going to happen immediately, then there's something that I've got to do about it, you see.

Yes.

Since this gradual percolation has been allowed for, it's nice to look at other things in the bookshops now instead of just the 'spiritual' section. It's nice to be relaxed enough to look at other things like novels and crafts and hobbies. So if there's a 'me' here, I think I'll just let it be, let the percolating happen.

Sounds good to *me*! (*laughter*)

July

East Sutton, Kent

One-Day Retreat

There's something else going on, when you talk, and there are spaces between the words. There is this spaciousness that takes over, and it's hard to concentrate on what you're saying. There's a tendency to think that that stillness is actually the true nature, but is it just another experience?

In the absence of 'I' there is 'stillness'. 'I' reappears and claims stillness as an experience. In fact there is only experienc*ing*, know*ing*, see*ing*—which is 'stillness', but is *also* the appearance of 'I' as part of the scenery in the play of life.

Therefore, stillness is not an experience, but neither is anything else. There is only experiencing—with no experiencer—which is simply 'what is'. And that includes any appearance of 'I' as the present configuration.

There is a tendency to want to hang onto that spaciousness.

Yes. But there may also be a noticing that when the wanting to hang on occurs, then the 'I' has already been assumed, rather than seen for what it is.

If the understanding arises, 'All there is, is what is manifest-ing in present awareness', where is the difference between that as an idea, as a theory, as an opinion, as a belief, as a faith, if you like, on the one hand, and on the other hand the knowing of that?

This knowing which *is* our true nature, permeating into the play initially as a reflection in thought, is what we call understanding. Understanding is an apparent process in the play of life, whereas knowing is this, in and *as* which the play appears. Knowing *is* oneness, devoid of any necessity for concept or meaning.

There is something here, in this body-mind, that increas-ingly feels that that's right, that 'experiences' that. But there's also something in here that says, 'Well, that could just be brainwashing because I expose myself to this a lot.'

This doubt is undermined in presence, with its two aspects of awareness and the presently arising con-tent, which cannot be negated. They require no belief. When the focus shifts from understanding and belief—which are part of the mesmerising with con-tent—then there is resting as presence. Which is only ever the case anyway, but simply goes unnoticed.

There may be noticing that there is awareness, that this whole mesmerising assumption of 'I' is the content appearing presently in awareness. There *is* awareness, right now, and the content of awareness arises integrally, simultaneously with it. No belief is required.

OK, so if thoughts arise here along the lines of 'Perhaps there is a soul, some sort of journey, some sort of spiritual evolution,' it's just the same as a thought arising like, 'I wonder if I left the handbrake on in my car.'

Yes. Except that the thought, 'I wonder if I left the handbrake on in the car' is a bit more useful than all the rest of it. You might go and check then, before it's ploughed into too many other cars!   (*laughter*)

Thoughts are just flowers in the garden really?

Yes. They are just part of the scenery.

They are just attributes of the organ we call the brain really.

No, no. No image gives rise to any other. That's assumed in the play.

So is the arising of thoughts just a complete mystery?

Yes, just as everything is a complete mystery.

Thoughts appear to be 'inside', whereas a tree appears to be 'outside'.

When the 'I' thought has been assumed and all other thoughts become 'my' thoughts, then rather than being seen as part of the scenery, as is the tree, they appear as integral to this body image. They seem to be 'inside'.

When the 'I' thought and all other thoughts are viewed objectively—as the tree is viewed—then they no longer seem internal. Internal to what? 'You' are not exclusively the body. Your true nature is oneness—no-thing and everything, awareness and content, which includes this body and all bodies, all images, thoughts, sensations. No inside, no outside—all appearing presently on the screen of awareness.

For you, when you have thoughts, or when there are thoughts—how would that differ from when I have thoughts? Do you see them as objects?

They arise in exactly the same way. However, when seen objectively as part of the scenery, their message is no longer taken seriously. They are just a story and they lose their mesmerising quality.

So you don't see them as 'your' thoughts?

The 'I' that would claim them as 'mine' is also a part of the scenery. There is simply this open awareness in which all images appear and disappear. As in your case.

So for you, there is no inside or outside?

In the same way that there is no inside or outside for 'you'.

But there appears to be.

Yes, it is appearance only. When thoughts are seen for what they are—including the 'I' thought—then the play is lived in an ordinary fashion, so that there is no longer concern with 'inside' and 'outside' and all the rest of it. There is simply presence, and the play unfolds. But it's no longer mesmerising, it's no longer taken seriously.

When you say, 'Things just happen', for me it appears that they are happening to a 'someone', and also that in some way I am instrumental in, for example, going and getting the car and driving. There is a felt sense of 'I'.

Yes. This felt sense of 'I' is the functional sense of being that arises in conjunction with bodily location for daily living in the play. The 'I' with which we are generally concerned here is the 'I' thought which, when assumed, is the basis for the psychological self-sense, which is the story of a life extended in thought, in time.

I can temporarily see that.

Yes, maybe this seeing comes and goes—this 'I' will likely continue to appear and disappear. That's the nature of the play of life. Maybe the 'I' disappears altogether, maybe it is simply seen through—all of this is the play.

Within the play there may be a move to inspect the 'I', whereby it is noticed that it is merely a thought, an idea; that this life of the character apparently extended in time has no actuality outside of the present. The present, or presence, is awareness and its content.

Well, we say 'awareness' but, of course, that is a concept as well.

There is awareness, right now. There is registering of the wall, of the body, of thought. This registering is what the concept 'awareness' points at. Awareness is devoid of all qualities, and so it gets overlooked. It is what is looking, registering, right now—the awareness aspect of your true nature. This registering and what is being registered are not concepts. They are present, obvious. No recourse to thought is needed.

So is it like almost getting a habit of inspecting the 'I'?

Within the play a 'habit' may arise of inspecting the 'I', but of course, the development of this habit is, in the play, simply the recognition of your true nature as wholeness permeating into the play in this way—as a story involving a character making an inspection.

And you are overlaying it with a story?

'You' *are* the story.

❀   ❀   ❀

After liberation …

There is no liberation.   (*laughter*)

After the true nature is realised, you …

It's always presently. There is no 'after' or 'before'—it's always presently. So let's just say, 'In the present recognition of our true nature.'

In the present recognition of our true nature … (laughter)

Notice the subtle ways in which speech arises as an outward extension of thought.

And it keeps us trapped.

Nothing can keep you trapped. Your true nature is oneness. Oneness is never trapped, but there are subtle ways in which thought and speech seem to promote immersion in the play, the mesmerisation.

I hear this talk now and it's all clear and it's recognised and it's great. And then the phone rings or I go out to dinner, and back I am in the 'I' again. Why isn't it more constant? I mean, I know it's there constantly, but the clouds of 'I', 'I', 'I', 'I' come thick and fast.

I hear from you, and from other people, that there is no need for practices—I don't actually do any but I am just re-inspecting that, because I feel hijacked most of the time. Is there anything efficacious for letting one's true nature be felt?

No. *(laughter)*

This 'I'—this 'I' thought that is piggy-backing all these other thoughts about bringing your true nature to the fore—all of this is a play, an appearance in or on your true nature. This play seems to be about the recognition of oneness, about relaxing into the ease of being—which is actually already the case anyway, but is simply recognised via the medium of the play.

I totally hear you, but my living isn't mainly like that. My living is mainly in forgetfulness with the clouds parting here and there. Many times a day, certainly, the light falls on this object which calls itself 'I', but when I go out there, my true nature is obscured.

This remembering and forgetting *is* the play. Maybe an ease arises as to whether 'I' is there or not. It is simply seen through when it appears. Not believed anymore.

So when it arises, you stop and take a look.

Maybe that happens as part of the play.

It's like something natural, like self-enquiry naturally occurs?

Yes, just as everything is naturally, spontaneously occurring. Maybe something called 'self-enquiry'—inspecting the 'I'—happens. But there is actually no one doing it.

When this message permeates into the play, seeking begins to subside and there is relief and ease. But there is no answer to the apparent problems appearing in the play. All the while there is the assumption that your nature is this 'I', there is the attempt to deal with problems and to sort it all out. And for every problem sorted, there will always be a further problem. It is only when this recognition of your true nature begins to arise that real peace or ease is revealed. All the 'problems' are still there, but there is no longer identification with them.

❀   ❀   ❀

So to use that analogy of a cinema screen again, you can watch all the problems on the screen but they are not your problems.

That's right.

The only thing is, when you watch a film you can still identify and empathise.

You can become completely involved, so they do *seem* to be 'your' problems.

So it's sort of like, if you are in the cinema, you get lost in it, you get involved in it.

Yes.

So you get completely taken up with it but sometimes you can sort of stand back and think, 'Hang on, I'm in a cinema.' Or someone unwraps a sweet or something and the crackling noise breaks the involvement.

That's right, exactly. That's all that's happening today. You have gone into the cinema and someone is constantly crackling sweet wrappers! (*laughter*)

So how can we remember to unwrap the sweets and crackle the wrappers?

'You' can't remember. 'You' is the mesmerisation that disappears when the wrapper crackles. Then there is a permeating into the play of the recognition of your true nature—while at other times there is immersion. The sweets are just unwrapped when they're unwrapped and there is no choice about unwrapping them.

I suppose the question is, what makes it permanent, as it were?

Nothing makes it permanent. Within the play the search for 'permanency' appears as the agitation that seemingly prevents this permanency. There's not anything that you are doing or anyone is doing. It's all happening spontaneously.

Is it possible to recognise our true nature by reading this in a book or by hearing it on tape, two thousand miles away?

Of course. There is no necessity to go into a room where a character is speaking in this way, but that can appear very helpful. The reading of all these books about non-duality and Advaita and all the rest of it doesn't appear within the play to have quite the 'edge' that being in an interactive situation has. From the point of view of the identified character in the play, the book may just get included as part of the story of 'I'. Maybe even, 'I am enlightened or awakened.'

Whereas when we are in the room, in the cinema, with the sweet wrappers crackling all day long, then it's not so easy for it to become part of the story as it may with a book. Here, there is always a direct reminding of your true nature. All the questions are turned back on themselves to point to oneness, to presence. All the questions tend to have this component of 'I' in them, but they're not answered from that point of view. The 'I' is always undermined in the direct and immediate pointing.

❁　　❁　　❁

This is the absolute simplicity of it: awareness and content, awareness and content, the two aspects of oneness, wholeness, presence, 'what is'. And this search for there to be a permanent remembering is the play.

And we confuse this with 'I am aware.'

Yes.

So 'I' is a natural part of the content?

Yes.

It's astounding when you read that apparently solid things are basically all space, just energy. But that's just another story, isn't it, another metaphor?

Yes, interesting, but the mesmerising quality of the play takes over again and there is involvement in a story about scientists and atoms.

But within the story, it's kind of fascinating that the ancient seers apparently saw what our scientists are discovering now. It's fascinating that knowledge is being rediscovered, within the story, thousands of years later. You think, 'How the hell did those guys see that, without any particle generators?'

Yes, it's so fascinating that it gets overlooked that this is a story arising presently; that all of this 'ancient history' is appearing presently as a story that has a mesmerising quality. There is a constant tendency to become fascinated with the play and to overlook the fact that the identification as 'I' is the basis for this wandering.

Sure, but some of the content is fascinating.

Of course, but the nature of this scene in the play of life here today is that reminding of your true nature is happening, whereby the mesmerising quality of the fascinating content of the play is seen through.

But if there is a distraction, then that is 'what is'. Is not distraction just as good as anything else?

104

That's right. The recognition of your true nature is not necessary, but we're talking here in the context of oneness appearing as a roomful of characters seeking oneness, so this theme of undermining the seeking is arising. At a meeting such as this, it's like a hole appearing in what we usually take to be reality. We could get involved with discussing all sorts of fascinating and distracting stuff and spend all afternoon immersed in it.

That wouldn't matter, would it?

It wouldn't matter at all but as soon as you'd snapped out of it and you found yourself on the way home, you'd probably think, 'Well, that was a swizzle.' (*laughter*)

Sometimes when you're really absorbed in doing something, some activity, you just lose all sense of self.

Yes, but it's not that *you* are absorbed—there is simply absorption.

But after, when you've come round as it were, you remember that you were absorbed.

The 'I' reappears.

So I suppose maybe you could say, 'Well, it would be nice to be absorbed.'

Yes, it tends to be that relief is usually sought from 'I' in some form of distraction within the play.

We are just as we are—that's what you're saying—and the 'I' is all part of that.

Yes, a natural part of the scenery. There's no need to be rid of 'I'—maybe it's simply seen through.

There is just seeing 'I' for what it is.

Yes, the tension of identification as 'I' appears as the motivation for distraction or escape. But when the 'I' is seen for what it is, then the play is lived presently. Sometimes there is discomfort, maybe.

And it's the discomfort that causes the whole set of 'I don't want this—I want something else. I want to move from A to B'; the desire to move out of this into something else.

Yes, discomfort arises, and whenever there is the assumption of 'I'—'I am in discomfort'—there is the movement for 'I' to escape.

But there's no way of doing so.

There is no one to escape; it's just an idea.

But why would awareness choose to forget itself so completely?

There is no reason for any of it, the same as there is no reason for the picture on the screen—it's simply there: a series of images, apparently forming a story, but merely a series of pictures strung together, appearing in awareness.

But for the play to work, there has to be complete immersion in the play or story, because if there is half immersion, it won't work.

It's not that the play works or doesn't work. There is simply everything, as it is. There is awareness of the content of awareness. The content of awareness happens to be a play about seeking for wholeness. Awareness isn't actively forgetting itself, but there is a story in the play—being registered by awareness—about forgetting and remembering.

What you speak of as half immersion can be a feature of the play, whereby there is recognition of your true nature as oneness and yet, within the play, particularly compelling scenes arise (pleasure or suffering perhaps) and there seems to be either a lack of motivation or an inability for the 'I' to be entirely seen through.

It would be a bit like watching East Enders *with all the cameras showing. It would be very difficult to take it seriously.*

Yes, that's right, that's a good way of describing what's happening at a talk such as this: the cameras are on show.

So in the play it's a bit like a process of discovery of the scenery, noticing that it is actually a stage set with props.

Yes, that's right. Everything is the scenery: all thoughts, all feelings, all visual images are the scenery.

So there's no point to any of it?

No. Consciousness appears as the characters having a conversation about being aware of awareness.
(*laughter*)

Is there still a mystery for you?

There is simply 'what is'. Everything is a complete mystery. There is no secret hidden knowledge held here—there is simply the registering of everything as it appears. Just as it is in your case. But in some characters there is more 'in and out' of the mesmerisation. When the play is seen for what it is, all is still a mystery and maybe life just continues in the story mostly as it's always been. But the absence of seeking has a certain ease associated with it.

Ramana Maharshi lay on a couch for fifty years.

You're making it sound pretty inviting!   (*laughter*)

Thank you for all your excellent questions today, pretending to be seekers.

It's not difficult! (laughter)

I can see through your disguise, though.

Thank you for not giving us anything.

You're welcome.

The Lady from the Cowboy Movie

One of the main things I wanted to talk about was the fact that I do see this and the question is, if I really see this, then why don't I see this? You know what I mean? I really do see the awareness and I really ...

Who is really seeing this?

There is seeing.

There is seeing, yes.

There is seeing ... Often—well, often is not half the time or anything like that, but it's often enough—there is seeing of this.

Yes. So we could say there's remembering and forgetting; identification and disidentification.

Yes, but there are so many 'Ah-ha's' that it feels like, if it is being seen, then why doesn't it kick on over?

For whom? When you say 'Why doesn't it kick on

over?', there's automatically the presumption there of the separate 'I' again. Whereas when you say 'There is seeing', that's seeing as your true nature, isn't it?

It is. Then the thought arises that there should be something more.

Yes, the thoughts appear as part of the content and the thoughts appear as a story, don't they? 'There should be something different here.'

'There should be more.'

Because of the drama of the whole 'enlightenment' thing, we're led to believe that there's some great, fantastic experience to come.

Or even a subtle one, but something better than this.

Yes. Always looking for something more than what is. These kinds of experiences, events, do arise but they only arise in this awareness that's already the case now.

Yes.

They are simply a different configuration of the content. So there is already awareness and the content of awareness, and arising presently in the content of awareness are thoughts—thoughts perhaps of a subtle dissatisfaction with this content, a feeling that it should be different in some way. And that's the thought story, the engagement with the thought story, the mesmerisation.

So . . . notice that, basically?

'*You*' can't notice that, but it may be noticed.

Yeah, there's no control, is there?

No, it's all arising entirely of its own accord.

You said at the last talk it seemed to be that there is this exhaustion of seeking.

Maybe in some cases, but there doesn't necessarily need to be an exhaustion of seeking. There could be an immediate complete dropping of this separate self-sense. It's not dependent at all upon any exhaustion of seeking or anything like that.

Oh, good! (laughter)

All these stories arise that the character has to become exhausted and go into the desert and there's the dark night of the soul and all the rest of it. It's all completely a story, an absolute myth. Maybe something like that will happen—maybe not.

Already, right now, there is awareness and the presently arising content. And there may be focus and concentration on the thought story that's arising as part of the content, which *seems* to distract from this simple recognition of awareness and content ... But it's only a story. There is only ever presence.

Yes, there's the seeing of that. That really undermines the 'I' anyway, doesn't it?

Yes, there is seeing that the 'I' is a story appearing as part of the content.

Can I content myself in the meantime with the idea that there is apparent unfolding?

Well, this is back into the story as the 'I' again.

Yeah. God, it's so hard not to slip back into it.

This apparent struggle is part of the play, the story, happening automatically. Maybe it continues—maybe as part of the play it is seen through in some way: a sudden falling away of the 'I', or the inspection of the 'I'. There's no necessity to any of it, though.

The hardest thought stories that come up are the ones where you think that you will be trapped—that you will be the one who doesn't get it, who doesn't see it.

The play is on autopilot, including all of these arising fears and anxieties about it not being seen. I'm simply pointing out that there's only already awakeness, only already oneness, and maybe a story running about not getting it.

Yeah ... (sighing) I know. (laughter) Can you talk a

little bit about this waiting for confirmation of awakeness that you mentioned in Clarity*?*

A lot of characters turn up at the talks and there's a subtle waiting game for something to appear differently, for some kind of 'event' or experience as confirmation. But what confirmation is needed for presence? Awareness and the presently arising content—what confirmation is needed of that? It's the most obvious thing. If it's part of the character's story to be reminded in this way, then that's the way it is.

The part that I actually lose the easiest is the whole part about the 'I'. It isn't recognised where the 'I' is taking over.

Nothing's taking over. There is simply this play of movement in and out of identification. There is only awareness and the presently arising content, but there may be mesmerising, whereby the awareness aspect is overlooked in identification with the content.

I keep thinking that there's something I can do to undermine the 'I' a little more.

Well, as a happening, in this story, maybe some form of enquiry may arise, some form of inspecting the 'I'—but '*you*' won't be doing it.

OK. So it appears if it appears? It does seem to appear from time to time.

So when that arises, it happens. That's simply the story, isn't it? Consciousness in appearance as the character, involved with this game of inspecting the 'I' in some way. But there's no particular importance attached to that—apart from in the story as the character.

It's just noticed. Everything is noticed, I guess. And the noticing itself is recognition, again.

Yes. The play is seen through, this identification as the character is seen through. So there's no need for anything to change or disappear in any way whatsoever. There is still appearance as the character. We are not suddenly lifted out of this play in some magic display or other.

I don't look for that, but I guess I do look for experiences that I've read other people have had.

Well, within the play, that's the constant enticement, isn't it?

Yeah.

Consciousness is appearing presently as every character, and when these experiences are spoken or written about, they appear as an enticement for distraction within the story—'out of' presence.

I've read that when you're seeking and waiting, the waiting game is the 'last gasp'.

Maybe, but within the play, the hearing and accepting of that is another subtle little game of distraction. That is the certification of the seeking and waiting game: 'Oh yes, you are at present in the seeking and waiting game.' But that could go on for five weeks or it could go on for fifty years.

Yeah, it'll probably be fifty years for me! I'll be dead by then.

This focus on the seeking and waiting game is again another distraction. It's a subtle hanging on.

It's very hard, isn't it, with the words? I mean you do the best you can. I'm sure from your standpoint even it's hard. I mean, I know there's some slippage with everybody, but it gets to where you recognise the slippage too yourself.

Yes, many of the characters who turn up at the meetings are extremely sharp. This message has to be fairly precise. Fluffy meanderings about 'the truth' and 'enlightenment' don't wash these days.

But in a way it's almost like we know too much. You know what I mean? It's like there isn't anything else. There was all this brand new information, but now it's like there's nothing new left that can be said. How much clearer can you get, really?

Yes.

Now you're looking for the clearest of the clearest of the clearest of the clear. Oh God!

This is the nature of the seeking game in the play of life: always overlooking what's most simple and obvious in the focus on looking for something more. What we're talking about here is very simple but is served by precise expression.

Exactly. The seeking for something more seems endless. In the States there are new terminologies coming in like 'They're really laser' or 'They're really crisp.'

(*laughing*) Really? I've never heard those before.

This waiting thing: that's an interesting trap that I haven't really thought about till now.

Well, any kind of waiting implies something still to come, some future projected happening. There is only presence, in which this waiting game is happening. There is already presence: awareness and the presently appearing content. It cannot be negated. Nothing is required for presence. It's all there is.

It is important, I think, to keep hearing that, because it's so easy to forget. I'm sure that reading it can be a good reminder too.

Of course. There's not even a requirement that you come into the presence of a character where this reminding happens. There's no absolute requirement for it. Reminding may happen via a book or in endless other ways.

Hmm, that doesn't happen very often. Have you ever heard of it happening?

It tends to be that with the 'live' interaction, as it were, there's less of a chance of the subtle games carrying on. With a book, a story can be made around the contents. When there is the happening of the character, coming into the room and asking questions and those questions being continually undermined, it's much harder for a story to appear out of that. The living presence is not accommodating in that way.

I guess that's the resonating: that you're in tune with it in some way without being consciously aware of it. I think it's like when two tuning forks start being in tune with each other.

Right, sure, but let's not make anything special out of that either. It could be that you're in tune with a book or in tune with a vandal breaking up a bus-shelter or something like that. That could be it. There's no requirement for any special kind of circumstances for it at all, for this recognition.

Yeah, but it seems so clear when there is this continual reminder.

The thought story is being continually undermined. All of this seeking—this wandering around trying to get it—is a story. Right now, what is there? What thought story is there to mesmerise? There is simply a room with two characters; awareness and the presently arising content. There is an awareness right now, a registering, and there is what is being registered. This is presence, oneness.

The thought story is very compelling. You want to go with it.

Yes, the mesmerisation seems to distract 'away' from presence. But there is only ever presence. In this recognition, the thought story is undermined, seen through.

Yeah, absolutely. It is. Right now, presence seems very strong. There's a very strong pull towards it.

It's not that there's a very strong pull towards it. There is no pull towards anything. It simply is.

OK, the recognition is clear.

Yes.

Or the mesmerisation is pulling back or something.

Yes. The mesmerisation is not there at these times.

Yeah.

It's seen through.

Yeah, I think that's what's happening when I'm at these talks, the all-day talks especially. The recognition is there a lot.

Sure, yes.

Then there is the thought that I need to be by myself, for quiet time alone.

Yes, of course. It's OK to be at the talks and it's OK to be on your own or wherever. This remembering happens. It's not something that *'you're'* doing. No special circumstances are required.

No. Most of the time it appears just to come in like the tide ... But sometimes, it still feels like I've done something.

Sure, maybe as part of the story there is the apparent movement as the character in the play to inspect the 'I', to do some form maybe of enquiry or whatever it is that is the reminding. But it's only apparently so, because everything is happening entirely spontaneously. The appearance of this 'I'—everything that happens—is entirely spontaneous. It's only from the point of view of this 'I' that it is claimed as '*I* am doing something. *I* am doing enquiry. *I* am inspecting the I..' Whereas, in fact, everything is simply happening.

Like attention. That's a big one that seems to be related to the 'I': there seems to be a conscious choice about where you put your attention.

Yes.

But you can say 'Attending happens.'

Yes. As another word for 'attention', let's say 'seeing'. So sometimes there is simply seeing, and sometimes there is apparently seeing as the character.

Now what do you mean by that?

There is actually only ever seeing, but at times there is the play of identification as the character - so it seems as though the *character* is seeing, doing, all the rest of it. This is the mesmerisation. The thought comes up 'I am seeing'; 'I am doing self-enquiry' or whatever; 'I am reminding myself in some way.' Whereas in fact there is simply see*ing*, there is simply remind*ing*.

So you're trying to do self-enquiry or ...

No, '*you*' aren't—there's no 'you' ever doing anything—it's just a happening. The 'you', the 'I' is all part of the happening in the play.

It's so good to remember. That's so simple too—really, you've got it down to a science! (*laughter*)

It's just the way it comes out. Nathan can't claim any of that. Nathan is only another appearance the same as 'you' are.

Yes.

The same as all these characters. We're all the very same one. It just happens that it's the function of the

Nathan image to speak in this way.

Well, it amazes me how clearly it comes across. The whole teacher thing is the biggest story I have about the waiting, this idea about the teacher.

Consciousness is only ever having this conversation with itself. There is no 'other'. There is the appearance of 'many', but it's all the very same one, speaking as all these mouths, listening as all these ears, looking as all these eyes.

OK, I have a feeling that you're not going to answer this directly but, in your experience, was there a recognition that occurred with particular teachers?

If we want to make a story out of it—in the case of the character, Nathan, there was a gradual unfolding in the play. The struggling became less, the remembering became more frequent. It became obvious that there is no awakening—there is only already awakeness, in which this story of this unfolding recognition is appearing.

And then that was recognised by this character.

No. The character doesn't recognise anything—the character is what is seen through.

Right, yes. So it was all very subtle for you, yes?

Yes, just as it tends to be where most of these characters are concerned, this play of seemingly gradual unfolding where the character is seen through. It's more uncommon for there to be a sudden recognition or dropping of the 'I', where the 'I' no longer reappears.

OK. That's good. I'll hang onto that.   (laughter)

Nobody's hanging onto that! Still, it's nice, within the play, to have a little consolation.   (laughter)

Within the play, there is seeking and understanding, and even as the identified character, that understanding can bring a great sense of relief—the undermining of all of the ideas about all of this stuff the 'I' has to do.

Yeah, well, it is so pleasant for most of the time if you can have this consolation that everything is unfolding just exactly the way it should be; that it's all perfect. You don't get quite so caught up.

Sure.

I recognise the trap in it too.

Yes, if we can call it a trap—only within the play can we call it a trap. We can say that there is still this identification as 'I': 'I am seeking', 'I am understanding'. In the seeing through this, in the seeing through of the 'I', it doesn't mean that there has to be the disappearance of the 'I', but in the seeing through of it, immediately understanding is obsolete. There is no further need for consolation. At times, there may be a drifting back into the identification and so, at those times, the seeking and understanding game is played, and then there's a remembering and again this seeking and understanding game is seen through.

Does that appear to happen for a progressively less length of time?

So here's the 'I' wanting to be consoled again! Shall I say it goes on for two minutes or thirty years?
    (*laughter*)
There's six billion different possibilities here. It could last for a day, it could last for three weeks, or however long. Within the play there's plenty of capacity for distraction and plenty of capacity for remembering.

So just keep noticing that - then you're almost always there.

There is only ever presence, so there's nowhere to get to. The 'getting there' is the play.

You're only ever there but just not recognising that you're there.

That's right, yes.

I do have this thing about trying to find meaning in it all sometimes.

There's no meaning to any of it whatsoever, but that's part of the play, that we're constantly looking for special happenings and meanings and trying to figure it out. We find a certain crystal in a certain shop at a certain time ... and all the rest of it. That's fine—it's happenings within the play, but it's only a play.

Yeah.

I've got a whole pile of crystals over there!   (*laughter*)

Well, I do tend to do that. That's just a distraction, though, isn't it?

Well, when this story is seen through, even when it's no longer a distraction, it's still nice to look at crystals. That's the play. What else is there to appear as apart from this play?

Well, yeah.

There's just this ordinary life as the character, except there's the absence of tension, this wound-up spring that you've probably heard me talk about before.

With recognition, is there a lessening of wanting to get out and 'do' in the world?

It's different with every character. There is no longer the agenda, of course, but there may be a story arising whereby the character is seen through but the life of the apparent character is busy.

Has a busy life?

It could be so, yes. Or it could be that the character just likes to sit and look at the view.

Yeah, I could see myself doing a lot of that actually. (laughter)

Well, do it now.

I do. I've heard that laziness is very close to enlightenment.

Sounds fine. *(laughter)*

Do you feel that you're literally being lived through - are you aware of that?

There is only oneness appearing *as* every character, not 'through' every character—that implies a subtle kind of separation. These two characters sitting here is the present configuration of oneness.

And there's nothing else other than that.

That's right. There is only this.

Hmm. And if you were to get up and leave the country, for example, and start travelling around or whatever, there wouldn't be a sense that in some way you're watching yourself?

No, there is simply the living *as* this character.

And the story's no longer there.

There is this unfolding of the life as a character, but there's no investment in a past story or a future story. There is present unfolding, just as there is in the case of every character.

There is no difference. In fact, you don't know what's going to happen—anything beyond what's right here, right now.

No. There is only presence. There is nothing that is *going* to happen—all is presently happening, the same as it is in the case of every character. But where the 'I' appears, there is projecting into a future when something *will* happen, when there will be 'enlightenment' or 'awakening' or a wedding or a new car or whatever. And there is a projecting into a past—the life of this character as a child and growing up and all the rest of it.

And memory is this story of the past?

Thoughts arise that carry a 'memory' label, the content of which seems to refer to an earlier version of this character. But it's only a story, of course, that's arising presently. There is *only* presence, which maybe has a mesmerising focus in a memory story.

It seems that some things are more distracting than others.

Yes, arising as the content of awareness there are all kinds of images, including visual images, thoughts, sensations, feelings that we label 'emotions'. When this story gets very compelling is when there's not just a little thought story trucking along, but when—simultaneously with the thought story—feeelings are appearing. These are very compelling, seemingly entangled with the thought story. Seen objectively, though, there is a thought story comentary with feelings appearing simultaneously alongside.

And yet the thought comes first?

No, not necessarily.

I thought the feeling was a result of a thought.

No. Nothing is the result of anything else. All these images are appearing and being registered presently. One doesn't lead to another—that's the mesmerisation. There is only the arising of these separate images, which *appear* to create each other and which *appear* to be entangled.

But let's say we can disentangle them and put the thoughts on the back burner for the moment; take the thoughts out of the picture and leave the feeling. All that appears then is something like a sensation—maybe seemingly arising in the stomach area, and then perhaps being expressed via sobbing or in some way in some other part of the body. But without the simultaneous thought story, it doesn't usually hang about very long. In fact, it's only the thought story that appears to extend it 'out of' presence, into duration, to which the label 'suffering' gets attached. An endlessly distracting story.

In the seeing of these images objectively, though, they lose their mesmerising nature. Powerful feelings may still arise but without the capacity for distraction. The thought story that arises with them is seen for what it is.

And there is nothing separate watching it?

No, there is this appearance *as* the character, but the story of this character is no longer taken seriously. Life is lived as the character, but there is no longer the same investment. There doesn't have to be a 'final' and 'complete' seeing through, as such—maybe there is a gradual unfolding of this seeing and less investment in the story.

Life gets easier.

Yes, there is more of an ease.

And that's sufficient.

Yes.

Is there any forgetting for you, at this point?

There's no longer any concern about forgetting. There's no longer an investment in the play. The play unfolds but the story loses its mesmerising capacity.

The play is unfolding?

The play of life unfolds, but there's no movement to do anything about any of it any more. When there is recognition of our true nature, that oneness or Consciousness is presently appearing *as* this character, there's no walking around saying, 'I am Consciousness appearing as this character'—there is simply an ordinary life.

But even if there are health problems?

Or apparent difficulties, whatever, sure.

It's back!

What's back?

The remembering. (laughter) When the remembering is occurring, then of course there are all these very pleasant things associated with it.

Yes, ease. Maybe even blissfulness for some characters.

The play is very interesting.

Well, when it's seen as a play, with no longer the same personal dilemmas around it all, it is interesting, yes, of course. It's a show, isn't it?

It is a show. It is.

Still appearing in the show as the character and yet

without the same investment of trying to 'get' somewhere or to 'get' something.

That's right.

It's always right here, right now: awareness and the
presently arising content. Right now there is registering and there is a room with two characters being
registered. That's it. Then maybe thoughts arise, and
if they're not seen through, there is mesmerisation in
the whole thought story.

If I could just remember this.

'You' can't remember it, but it may happen that it's
remembered.

*I have no more questions. When you think about it, you
could see how there really couldn't be any questions. I mean,
asking all the questions is just a way of coming to the fact
that you don't have any more questions.*

Exactly, yes. So, in fact, there are no answers to the
questions, as such. The answers that are given to the
questions aren't direct answers to the questions—they
are actually an undermining of the questions.
    When the question comes out, from the point of
view of the identified character involved with the
search, they are generally about this 'I', about how it
will become enlightened in some way or how it can
get over some difficulties within the play. Whereas, in
fact, it's the very undermining of all these questions,

the pointing to this that already is, which is prior to the play as 'I' but also appears as the 'I'. Then that coiled spring unwinds—the questions fall away. Life is as it is.

The questioner and the questions become one.

They are already one.

That's right!   (laughter)

Kensington, London
Afternoon Talk

Nathan, when we say 'our true nature', there isn't in fact anything that isn't our true nature. Everything is our true nature because everything is Consciousness—even when there is an 'I' that says that it isn't or that there is something that one doesn't get.

Yes, it's being spoken of in this way here today because this little scene in the play of life—the appearance of this roomful of characters—seems to be about recognising that there is already one hundred percent awakeness. Most of the time, for most of the characters in the play, there is the assumption of being a 'someone'. Therefore, recognising our true nature as oneness cannot be a special or important scene because there are a whole lot more characters—a lot more 'someones'— watching the football today than there are in this room listening to this message.

With regard to the movie on the screen analogy that's often mentioned, there isn't a divine controller behind the scenes, switching the images on and off? It's just happening?

Yes. This movie is running of its own accord. The 'divine' *is* the movie. There is no entity behind the-movie, projecting it. The movie is the immanent appearance of oneness.

So in the movie, in the play, there is a distinction between the point of view of identification with the 'I' thought and that of seeing through the 'I' thought, in the sense that in the latter case there's freedom from the illusion of being bound to the content of awareness?

Yes, but it's not that there's any need to be rid of thought—it's just a part of the scenery. And when it is seen as such, then a natural ease arises.

But there has been the idea here that there would be a great change when the 'I' is seen through.

No, not necessarily so. In some characters there is perhaps a sudden recognition of the true nature as oneness, and then—maybe, but not invariably—there might be a blissfulness associated with that, a kind of exaggerated relief at the release of tension. More commonly, because the seeing through of the 'someone' in the play has been gradual, there has been a gradual release of the tension associated with being a 'someone'. And so there isn't much tension hanging around anyway—therefore there isn't necessarily any kind of great blissful release.

Nathan, I really enjoy hearing the way you speak about oneness, using your concepts of 'awareness' and 'content of awareness'. I've noticed, since I first heard this, that either there is undistracted awareness or suddenly I startle myself by noticing that I have been into a stream of thought. Would you talk again about noticing?

Well, this noticing—although it appears as part of this play, as seeming to be something that the character is doing—is in fact happening spontaneously. There is simply this presently arising recognition of your true nature. Maybe the 'I' comes and goes, and maybe noticing happens.

And all we do is to keep noticing the awareness and the content of awareness.

'You' don't keep noticing it—as just mentioned, it's happening spontaneously.

It's just noticed. No one is noticing.

Yes. What initially arises as understanding in the play dissolves in knowing, and there is no longer any need for analogies or understanding of any kind. There is the direct, immediate, thought-free recognition of our true nature.

The old tool-bag gets left behind at some stage.

Yes, and there is the recognition that there has only ever been wholeness or oneness.

❀   ❀   ❀

Somehow the mind gets tired and there are no more questions. The mind gets tired—but there is no mind?

There is no mind.

How does it get tired?

There is no mind, so it doesn't get tired. In this play, maybe the apparent stream of thoughts (which you are referring to as 'mind') seems to be less mesmerising; the play is seen through, and there is resting as oneness. Although it may seem that it has arisen as a process in the life of the character, the 'someone', in fact there has never been a life of the character. That's just a story, and Consciousness or oneness has only ever been present, completely, already awake. This recognition of our true nature arises as a scene in the play. There is only the play *in* and *as* which to appear.

So the thought 'The mind gets tired' is just another concept.

Yes, immersion in the stream of arising thoughts is what is referred to as mind, but when it's seen through, mind is obviously a phantom.

Now there's no need to get rid of thoughts, of course—it's simply recognised that they are a natural part of the scenery. There is a knowing that the apparent stream of thought is actually only single thoughts appearing and disappearing, just as the propeller appearing to be a circular entity is actually single blades. There is no actual solid entity there. But when not seen objectively and given a name such as 'mind', the apparent stream of thoughts is seen as 'my' mind ... 'my' life, 'my' story.

The great epic.

It all becomes very obvious. If we started talking here today about so-called awakening as something that could happen in the future, as something which Nathan has (awakeness) and which isn't already the case in Consciousness's appearance as *every* character, then awakening becomes a golden carrot, continually dangled ahead of us. A future projected awakening appears, in the play, to promote mesmerisation, the continuing immersion in thought as the psychological self-sense.

There is also this idea that there should be something 'other-worldly'.

Yes, other-worldly is another projection, isn't it, because other-worldly isn't appearing as the present content of awareness—it's just an idea, a thought. There is no other world. There is only the constantly changing configuration of the present content of awareness.

It's not to say there isn't ...

Anything can arise in awareness. Any 'realm' can arise, but it will just be a different display of images appearing presently as the scenery.

Would it be fair to say that you have to recognise the ordinary before you see the extraordinary?

No, it wouldn't be fair to say it. *(laughter)*

I thought you might say that.

There are no qualifications whatsoever.

There is just what is.

Yes.

❀   ❀   ❀

Nathan, is there any curiosity in you about what happens when your body dies?

The body is appearing presently and it isn't 'dead'. Preoccupation with death is a diversion from presence. We could in the play have an entertaining conversation about death, but all the while the 'I' is assumed and goes unexamined, then conversations of this nature tend to be about 'my' death as a future projected event that will happen to an identified character. Your true nature is oneness.

Sometimes I think that this body seems to have access to a kind of wisdom which my mind doesn't seem to have access to.

The body doesn't know anything about death—the body is a present appearance in awareness.

So there is no such thing as the body having its own kind of wisdom?

Yes, but it's present—it's not related to time. What you're calling 'mind' is only the apparent stream of thought. So all of this stuff with regard to death and all the rest of it are all just thoughts that are arising presently in awareness. Of course, if there is immersion in thought, then there are all sorts of curiosities and a future is invented in which there will be death. But all there is is the present. There is presence, awareness and content, with a conversation about death happening. If these questions are entertained, we're just playing around in thought. In a meeting such as this, there is a constant reminding of our true nature, and the thought stories are seen through as they arise.

And so the question and the questioner are just thought.

The questions arise from focus in the thought story.

And we just notice this.

There is the noticing, presently.

Presumably part of the noticing is that things appear to change. And that—if I'm not mistaken—is the paradox: that the mind creates psychological time as an explanation for things appearing to change.

Everything is changing: that is the nature of the play, of the content of awareness. But there is no mind to create anything. There is awareness and the presently appearing content, including thoughts which *appear* to constitute a mind. These thoughts are information about a non-existent past and future which give the impression of duration—the extension 'out of' presence.

Is there any explanation of the apparent paradox that things appear to change but there is no time?

All there is, is the ever-moving, changing content, arising presently in awareness. It's only when there is immersion in the stream of thought that time seems real. In presence there is the knowing that what is appearing, presently, as a life apparently extended in time is the play of life.

❀　　❀　　❀

It seems like it's easier seeing the objects in your visual awareness as objects, but much harder to see the psychological self-sense and body as just the content of awareness.

Yes. With the appearance of the body in the play, there is an associated functional sense of self, but this may be differentiated from the psychological self. It is this psychological self which gives a sense of separation from all else that appears, such that this body becomes 'my' body.

This country is new to me so I find that I'm more self-conscious about things that I wouldn't otherwise be conscious

*of—'Am I doing or saying culturally acceptable things?', for
example. They're all concepts and ideas, of course, but it
seems like it's more obvious, more extreme, I guess I should
say—a more extreme example of how we're constantly
developing that sense of self just from our own ideas.*

Yes, it can be that when unusual circumstances arise in
the play, there is more of a tendency towards immersion in the stream of thought.

*In some ways it's easier because I feel like this is a play. I
feel like I'm in a Dickens novel, and if you came to where
I live, you'd feel like you were in a grade B cowboy movie.
So it seems more like a play, in that sense.*

An. Q: Any particular novel? Hard Times? *(laughter)*

So there is awareness of the ever-changing, moving
images. And sometimes there is immersion in the
story, overlooking our true nature as wholeness, as
oneness, and there appears to be this fractionating,
this dividing, this separation, whereby we take ourselves to be a 'someone', a 'something', instead of nothing and every-thing. This appearance of a 'someone'
is a play—there is only ever no-thing and every-thing,
oneness. There is no particular significance to immersion as a 'someone' or to seeing through the 'someone',
but from the point of view of the 'someone', it seems
to make a difference. Even when there seems to be a
'someone', there is actually only complete awakeness,
but our true nature as wholeness is overlooked. When
our true nature is recognised, then 'someone' still
continues to appear but is seen through.

What sees through it?

There is simply seeing—there is no-thing, no one that sees.

There is no-thing and no one that seeks understanding?

There is simply seeing, knowing.

Seeing through or not seeing through—there is just seeing?

Yes. The 'someone' is always looking for some significant change to confirm so-called awakening. But there is only already awakeness, which may or may not be recognised. The search for awakening by the 'someone' is always projected in time, but no awakening can possibly ever happen because there is only ever awakeness. Without awakeness, none of this could appear.

Sometimes I think that those people completely identified in the play, if asked a question about life, would say, 'Oh, this is just as it is.' I was on a retreat where some people from the retreat went to the local pub and someone in the pub asked them 'What are you doing there at that nice house?' The people replied, 'Oh, we're asking the question "Who am I?"' To which the man in the pub said, 'Well, you are who you are!'

Within this play there is the appearance of 'someone' and in most cases there is no questioning of that. There is no need for there to be any questioning of it—Consciousness is all that is, with no requirement of recognising its true nature. Recognising your true nature is not an advantage—that is the seeker's assumption and is what *appears* to keep the whole seeking drama in place, the idea that there will be an advantage.

So everything is OK as it is?

Yes, there is no need for there to be a recognition of your true nature. This is a play without necessity.

Often I wonder if those people in the pub are closer to it than us. That can't be so because it is all Consciousness, but often 'ordinary' people seem happier than spiritual seekers.

Yes, that often seems to be the case. In the play, though, where there is no explicit search for wholeness, then seeking for wholeness arises in other forms: seeking for material fulfilment, for example, or all the other endless ways that characterise life in the play.

So it's all just seeking, whatever the goal of seeking is?

Yes, that's right, that's the nature of the play. Within the play, though, when there is identification as the character, as 'someone', and the 'someone' isn't being seen through, then there is an accompanying tension, the wound-up spring that is *apparently* driving the character in the play. As the seeking is dissolved in knowing, in the recognition of wholeness, then the tension naturally unwinds and ease or peace is revealed. There seems to be, in this ease, an ordinary life, but it's an ordinary life free of tension, no longer dominated by acquisition and desire. All that is seen through.

Which is what is so extraordinary.

Yes, but when there is seeking from the point of view of the identified 'someone', the extraordinary is sought rather than the ordinary. So presence is always being overlooked in identification with content. Oneness— no-thing and every-thing—is overlooked when there is immersion as something or 'someone'.

Immersion as 'someone' sometimes gives the appearance of being reduced in meditation. Is that an illusion? Are there degrees of being immersed or not immersed? Does it have an on or off?

It's not that there are degrees of being immersed, although it appears that way. There is initially, perhaps, sporadic recognition of our true nature permeating into the play, which seems gradually to become more continuous. Meditation doesn't necessarily have anything to do with any of that at all. In meditation there can be the slowing down or the ceasing of the arising thoughts, but when meditation is finished, then the thoughts tend to reappear.

So the stopping of the arising thoughts is of no contribution to recognition?

No, thoughts are a natural part of the landscape and it doesn't matter if they arise or not. In the present recognition of your true nature as wholeness, then thoughts probably continue to arise—including the 'I' thought—but they are seen through. If there has been a tendency in the case of this particular character to meditate, then that is likely to continue. If there has been a tendency to be a footballer or a piano player or whatever, then that continues. It's simply that there is knowing—*as* your true nature—that permeates the play, which allows—or is—the ease or peace that was previously sought.

Does there tend to be an accompanying radical aliveness? Sometimes words of that kind have been used—like an energetic quickening or something?

Maybe, maybe not—anything can arise. In the case of some characters, there may be a sudden dropping of the self-sense and perhaps blissfulness arises, 'radical aliveness'... whatever name we give to whatever *is* in the absence of the tension of seeking. Unless the play has been seen for what it is, though, then sooner or later there is a return to the play of identification as the character, or a moving in and out of identification. It is, of course, also possible that there could be a sudden recognition of your true nature that is continuous. Far more commonly, though, there is a play of gradual recognition, so that there need not be any blissfulness or 'radical aliveness' or any other accompaniment that stands out particularly. Ease and well-being are enough. To simply see that there is always and only presence doesn't need to involve any radical experience or event.

So how to drop those expectations?

You don't drop them. As the unfolding story of the character in the play, they are maybe gradually dropped.

Oneness or wholeness has already been the case all along—it's merely that it's been overlooked. There has only ever been awakeness, simply not recognised. So with this continual reminding of your true nature, then the thoughts that arise as questions are seen through and need no answers. There is still the appearance of the character but it is presently seen through, and tension subsides.

Is there a sense that our true nature is profoundly related to love, or is that another thought?

In the absence of tension, the ease of being may be interpreted as love or 'unconditional love', or we could call it 'strawberry yoghurt'. Whatever is revealed as what we are referring to as ease needs no special name. From the point of view of the identified character in the play, grand names for the ease tend to promote a focus on the extraordinary—as a 'someone' *seeking* unconditional love, bliss or whatever. In the absence of the tension of seeking there is what presently is.

So when this incredible force of love hits you and knocks you for six, it has no more nor less significance than the rain falling on this house?

Which incredible force of love is this that hits you?

It does sometimes; it seems that there is a happening. I don't want to attribute anything to it, but it seems that it's happening more to this seeker, whereas it didn't when there wasn't the seeking.

Yes.

So are they other plays of the mind or are they just happening and that's it?

What you are calling this incredible force of love is simply the present configuration of the play for your particular character. Consciousness appears as every character and it's different in every case. So what is experienced in one character as 'an incredible force of love' hitting may in another character be a simple sense of ease or well-being, with no force of love or any other particular association. It can even be that when very compelling experiences arise, they tend to promote continued immersion.

A diversion.

Yes, a desire for more of it. But what is always presently the case, whatever is appearing as the play? There is simply awareness and content, presently, whether there is love or apparent suffering.

One more thing to slip up on.

Yes, this 'I' thought is a tricky customer, very slippery in its subtlety, constantly seemingly diverting attention into immersion as the stream of thought, 'away' from presence—which needs no particular sensation or experience but *is* all sensations and experiences, including the apparent diversion 'away' from presence.

And you just gradually become more and more aware of that—you don't make it a practice.

'*You*' don't become aware of that, but recognition emerges.

So focusing attention arbitrarily doesn't help?

If, for a particular character, the play of focusing attention is how oneness is revealed, then that's the way it is. But your true nature is always presently, immediately, the case—which could be revealed by countless different ways or by no way at all. Nothing whatsoever is required to be what you already are.

❀   ❀   ❀

It does seem a bit of a paradox that there is absolutely no merit at all in the recognition of our true nature.

Yes, there is only 'merit' from the point of view of the identified character.

So one sees that it's just part of the play that's going on in this room, at this moment.

Yes, but the character doesn't see it—it is seen by no one.

For which there's absolutely no merit?

No, that is the story, that there is merit; it's the play.

There is no seeker, there is no path?

No, only apparently so.

No excitement any more?

Maybe there is excitement or maybe not. Often what is meant by excitement is the hope of awakening or enlightenment, continually projected as a future event. The fix and rush of going to different meetings, getting a new book, searching for Nirvana ...

And yet there is here, sitting in this chair, a dissatisfaction arising as to what is happening at this moment, because of all one has been fed all one's life up until now—the expectations and the hopes and the path and the seeker and all sorts of scenarios. But actually, there's nothing. And that leaves a flatness ... Well, utter flatness actually, almost complete desolation. And it's not very nice.

What you're calling flatness is actually the peace and ease that's always been here but now it's minus the 'excitement' of seeking, hoping, pushing, advancing. Where this whole breaking down of identification as the character is happening, then maybe resting in being doesn't seem enough initially, and the flatness is a kind of grieving for that old high-seas, swashbuckling adventure of seeking.

The seeking is only ever for the ease that's always here, but there is immersion in the thrill-charged search *for* ease rather than resting *as* it.

With the breaking down of identification as the character, at times the 'I' is not completely seen-through, and along with the assumption of 'I' goes a sense of incompleteness, of not being whole. However, as soon as there's a movement to seek wholeness, that movement is seen through. Seeking for wholeness is no longer a possibility and the 'I' collapses again. This is what's sometimes referred to as being in the desert, the very idea of which becomes another focus in thought, a waiting game in the play. 'I'm in the desert': another version of seeking.

Everything you're saying—everything you've said this afternoon—sits very happily with me, but the heart is bereft. Recognition—you talk about recognition: intellectually, it sits very well ... And yet, if there have been any glimpses or moments, they have been felt in the heart. It just feels sterile, whereas before there have been various experiences of tremendous excitement and joy and love and all this sort of thing, and tremendous outpouring.

Yes, of course. All of this is the multicoloured play of life. When it's seen that *all* is simply, presently, arising scenes in the play, then everything is allowed: joy, love—and also flatness.

It's like a landscape and when the lushness disappears out of you, there's a desert. It's all just landscape, isn't it?

Yes, landscape is a good word for it. Sometimes the landscape includes joy, and sometimes it includes desolation; sometimes it's green and sometimes it's brown.

In the immersion in the play, the joyous experiences are seen as 'the answer', the escape, and the crap experiences are what we're trying to escape from.

Yes, exactly, whereas at each present moment that the immersion is seen through, then it collapses into awareness and content of awareness—wholeness, oneness, presence, 'what is'.

August

Kensington, London
Afternoon Talk

I had two experiences and they both lasted about a week. It seemed to me that there wasn't anything happening, that I was just that, and that was more than enough. It was like everything that I'd held onto and everything that had been important to me just seemed to collapse. It lasted about three or four days and I was just very light and relaxed, and I knew that all that was left for me was just to sit back and see it happening, see these things unfolding.

I guess there is nothing I can do or anyone else can do about it, but I just hoped that this experience would establish itself.

What you're referring to is actually the falling away of this sense of 'I' that we've spoken of. And when this falling away happens, where there is a sudden dropping of the 'I', then often there is a blissfulness, a release, associated with this. But usually, when these events arise where there is the falling away of the 'I', the 'I' then reappears and there is a sense of disappointment.

It tends to be the case that, coming to meetings of this nature, reading books about non-duality, etc, there is—within the play of life—a gradual dropping of the 'I', a gradual releasing of this tension, of identification as the character. And so the ease that is associated with the absence of the 'I' gently, gradually appears. These sudden disappearances of the 'I'—the sudden dropping, the seeing through of the mesmerisation—are very compelling. And so when the 'I' reappears, there is a searching for more of that, wanting to get back to the absence of the 'I'.

But all of this is happening spontaneously. No one is doing any of it. There is nothing that the 'I' can do to produce the absence of the 'I'. These events arise from time to time within the play of life, and they often appear as the stimulus for the seeking.

From the point of view of the identification as the 'I', it feels as though 'I'—this identified character—can do something about it. It seems that maybe it can do some kind of meditation or read certain books or go to a few extra meetings, whatever ... something to promote this dropping, this absence of the 'I'. But in fact all of this is happening spontaneously.

Yes, I didn't sit down and decide that I was going to drop the 'I'.

No, absolutely not. It happens spontaneously. It's very compelling, isn't it?

Yes, but not only that—I don't seem to have much interest in doing anything else but just being ...

... absent! *(laughter)*

154

When this happens—the seeing through of the 'I'—it kind of undermines this whole story that's being played here, the story of the life of the apparent character, where this 'I' must keep busy doing stuff, achieving and all the rest of it. Maybe a liking for simplicity—just hanging out—arises.

I keep hearing this voice laughing and saying, 'Stop pretending you're not already there!'

Sure yes, it tends to be that even where there has been a profound seeing through of the 'I', there is still a subtle waiting for the 'permanent' absence of it. But when 'I' is seen for what it is, then the appearance of 'I' is no longer a problem; it's a natural part of the scenery. There is the body image appearing and the 'I' thought is appearing simultaneously, and these images are being registered presently in awareness. Our true nature as oneness is never absent and the identification as 'I', as this character, is the play.

So there is nothing that this character can do to produce the absence of the 'I'. These events come and go. This is what we're referring to as the play of life. There is no prescription that can be given. This talk today is rather a description of what is already happening.

Yet surely it helps to have these reminders? Hearing constant reminders of our true nature at these meetings?

Within the play of life it appears that way. Within the play of life there is the coming to meetings or reading books, whereby this sense of separation, this 'I', this mesmerisation is gradually seen through.

When we really understand what you're talking about, is it that the 'I' can come back but you see through it, rather than it being the 'I' dropping off? When you understand what's going on, for want of a better way of putting it, is it that the 'I' can be absent or the 'I' can be present but it's understood?

Of course. Initially it may manifest as what we refer to as understanding, which is the reflection of knowing, the innate knowing *as* our true nature.

It's completely possible for the 'I' to be present and yet seen through. We're not looking for any sustained absence of 'I'. Such events may happen, but they aren't necessary. It's not necessary for the 'I' to completely disappear. If there is knowing as our true nature, then it doesn't matter what appears, whether there is the appearance of 'I' or the absence of it.

Is it that the constant interpretation of what's going on drops away?

It's simply that this mesmerisation where there is exclusive focus on the content aspect of oneness (traditionally referred to as *maya*), this sense of separation as the 'I', this disparity between innate knowing and apparent separation—it's seen through.

There is only ever oneness in its two aspects of awareness (or registering) and this that is presently registered. There is awareness right now, and there is the presently appearing content. That's all we're talking about here. As part of the content, the thought story appears, the belief in the past and future, the idea that this character may some day become enlightened or awakened. Whereas, in fact, there is only ever presently awakeness as oneness. There is awakeness—there is awareness right now, the registering of the images that appear as the content. That's all that's ever happening.

The oneness includes the character and the awareness?

Yes.

And as it's oneness, there's nothing that you can do about it—it's all Yourself?

Yes. This apparent separation as the character is the present play of oneness. Oneness appears presently as every character. The joke is that there is this roomful of characters talking about oneness, about the search for oneness—which *is* the immanent appearance *of* oneness *as* all of these characters.

The first time the event arose, I had to try and remember what you do in the morning. I really wasn't at all sure that I would be able to do my work. So I thought, 'I'd better do these things that you do in the morning and see what happens.' Once I couldn't remember how to cross the road. I mean, the whole thing was that it didn't matter—it didn't matter if I could work or not.

Didn't matter if you were squashed on the road! *(laughter)*

There was just this immanence that you're talking about.

There is only ever this immanence, but the mesmerising story is a seeming distraction from it, the story of a transcendent divinity, etc. It's only this immersion in the thought story that appears to extend 'out of' presence.

❀   ❀   ❀

Nathan, for the uninitiated, could you give a sort of overview of such basic questions as 'Who am I?' 'What is awareness?' 'What is the nature of this construct?'

Concepts are used to point to this which simply is. There is only Consciousness or oneness, which may be described as having two aspects—awareness and the content of awareness. All the images that appear as the present content are being registered in awareness. These images include visual images, thoughts, sensations, emotions, etc. And amongst the thought images, there is a primal thought image which is the 'I' thought. This 'I' thought appears to arise simultaneously with the body image.

When there is overlooking of the awareness aspect of our true nature and exclusive identification with content, this 'I' is assumed—'I am this character', and all other thoughts that appear become 'my' thoughts, 'my' life, 'my' story. This play as the identified character seemingly blossoms in this mesmerisation.

Maybe, as part of this play, there is recognition or acknowledgement of the awareness aspect, the registering aspect of our true nature. The mesmerising is seen through, and this 'I' and all other thoughts are seen to be appearing as part of the scenery. They have no particular significance over any other image.

When there is identification as 'I', there is a sense of separation and, simultaneously, the intuiting or innate knowing of our true nature as oneness. This disparity appears as tension or agitation, manifesting as the search to be free of 'I', to escape from 'I'. But there is no escape. 'I' is simply an image, and either the hearing of a message such as this or maybe the appearance in the play of some form of enquiry, some examining of the 'I', may appear to lead to seeing it for what it is.

But there is only already oneness, only already awakeness, whether there is mesmerisation as the 'I' or whether there is the seeing of it as merely another image.

The way you describe it, it sounds almost as if it's harder to maintain the illusion than the other way around.

Maybe so. There's no necessity for any of it. You could be sitting in the park eating a banana and the 'I' is seen through. You could be reading *Noddy and Big Ears* and there's a complete, total and permanent dropping of the 'I'. You could be playing football. There are no rules to any of it—no special requirements.

But isn't there a point in time when it's seen that this is it?

It's only seen presently, and presently it's seen that time is the story. So what appears as a time when there wasn't recognition is only a story being projected presently. There is only presence.

However well I see through the 'I', what I still know is that I feel separate.

This sense of separation is a functional aspect of the play, that this body appears as separate from that body; it's necessary for the play to function. There is presently a play of images—this image appearing here, that image appearing there. But it's seamless, it's all the same movie, the same picture. This functional sense of separation is bodily rather than psychological—the separation that we referred to earlier as the 'I' is psychological.

Could you explain what you mean by psychological?

With the identification as 'I', all of the other thought images become 'my' thoughts, and this seeming succession of thoughts is what is referred to as 'mind' or the psychological self-sense.

If we take the idea of a book—a complete story from beginning to end—it's all there now, in the present, but it takes the character a long series of occurrences to get through to the end.

Yes. That's a nice analogy.

It's difficult to get away from dualism, in words.

Yes, we can only use concepts, words, to point to what is. It simply is. *This* is it—there is simply this. In the seeing of the 'I' as a natural part of the scenery, then all of this use of concepts as pointers collapses into present living as oneness—which is already the case anyway. So there's no need to walk around saying 'Awareness and content—awareness and content' or anything like that. This life is lived *as if* there is past and future but they are simply seen through, with no longer any need for explanation.

Biddenden, Kent

A Visit to My Favorite Avon Lady

I want to ask a question about when there is present suffering. Although it may be acknowledged that the 'I' that seems to be experiencing the suffering is illusory, there is still, for example, present physical pain that feels unacceptable. Can you address that?

When the 'I' is seen through and there is pain, then that is the configuration of the presently arising play. Pain in a physical sense is a present sensation and tends to be less difficult when there isn't the projecting of it from the point of view of the 'I' into an imagined future. In that projecting, physical pain is accompanied by anxiety: there is a focus on thoughts that arise about its continuity—what we call suffering. The thought about it—the projection that this pain will continue into a future—becomes the extension of it, the continuation of it. Pain is a present occurrence, and in present living without extension into an expected future, it tends to be more manageable. Appropriate measures are taken within the play of life for its relief.

The pain, however, does seem to come up over and over and over again in the lifetime of the apparent individual. The mind does create stories and it happens like this (snaps fingers) *continually. So there is the suffering added to the physical sensation of what we call pain. That mental projecting into the future is very heavily imbued with the 'I', feeling anxious about future pain and so on. It seems such a solid identification.*

Yes, when the 'I' begins to be seen through in the unfolding of the recognition of our true nature, then this projection of pain into the future—which we're calling suffering here—begins to be undermined. However, this likely appears as a gradual happening in the play, so there is still the moving in and out of identification as the character and the consequent suffering. While this seeing through the play is unfolding, there's not necessarily any direct and immediate consolation or relief for that pain apart from what can be done in the play by way of medical treatment. For instance, if it's a headache, taking an aspirin ... With any physical pain, taking appropriate measures. That's all part of the play, and when it's seen in this way, as being a play, then this tendency to project it as a continuation into the future is undermined and makes physical pain seem more bearable. There is not the accompanying suffering, at least.

Could it be said it's almost as if there's a mental reminder of what you've just said to cut through this projecting into the future, which is the suffering tacked onto this present physical pain. What is this seeing through that you're talking about, though? Is it something that the individual appears to remember to do?

Appears to. Initially, from the point of view of identification as the character in the play, it certainly does appear as a process of remembering and understanding. There may be the reading of books, going to talks, and it seems from that point of view that the character is involved in this reminding. Awakening is projected as a future event where there is going to be the dropping of this bodily association and consequent release or bliss.

But we're not actually doing the reminding—is that what you're saying?

That's right. As the play unfolds and is permeated by knowing, then it is clear that this character is simply an appearance, a happening in the play, and the reminding and recognising of our true nature is all part of that. What initially appears as understanding dissolves into knowing, and it is seen that there is no awakening—there is simply awakeness; and that the play of identification as the character appears as a kind of a mesmerisation. The awakening that has been sought for is, in fact, rather the recognition, presently, that there is already awakeness.

When the mesmerisation as the individual character is happening, are you saying that during that time the awareness side of things is not predominant? Do you see what I'm saying? At the moment we seem to be talking of two things—the awareness and the content of awareness, and when there is identification as the content of awareness, then at that time the awareness side of things is absent. Is that what you're saying?

No, I'm saying that awareness is always present, but if there is mesmerisation and exclusive focus in the play as the character, the awareness aspect of our true nature is overlooked. There is still awareness registering the content of the play, but there is not the *recognition* of this registering. There is registering without the recognition. So there is focus in the play, in the content of the play, and that's what I've spoken of as being the focus as 'someone'. Whereas when there is recognition of our true nature, it is seen that our true nature (oneness) is no-thing—awareness; and it is also every-thing—the content of awareness.

On the one hand we're talking almost as if there's something wrong with the mesmerising aspect of this, and yet you are saying that it is all part of one big whole.

Yes, there's nothing wrong with the mesmerisation—that's simply the play. It's from the point of view of the identified character—the exclusive focusing on the content—that there seems to be something wrong.

Is that the suffering?

Yes, and within the play it appears as the motivation to escape *from* the play. In the context of what we are talking about today, it appears as seeking and trying to understand by the identified character or 'I'.

The knowing—which is our true nature—begins to percolate into the play initially in the form of this quest or desire for understanding to help with what are seen as the problems of life. However, understanding is simply the reflection of knowing arising in thought form. But because the nature of thought as part of the content of the play is ever-moving, changing, then the arising of knowing reflected as understanding—although relieving to the character—does not undermine the 'I'. It appears as something that the 'I' does.

In the continual reminding of our true nature—whatever form it may take—knowing is likely revealed and the 'I' is seen through, rendering understanding obsolete.

I want to ask something else now, and I'm aware that this is again talking from a sense of a separate 'I', but I'll ask the question anyway.

There's a growing sense that this body-mind struggles a lot with daily life, in the sense that there seems to be a pushing against a natural way of living. In other words, when the body-mind is tired it should rest, and yet so often it can't do that. It has to earn a living. It has to respond constantly to doing things to live a life. I look at the trees, I look at the flowers, I look at the animals out there, and they're able just to go with the flow and keel over and die when their time is up. But somehow, being a human being, living in this world, it seems we have to force the body-mind to live in a way that doesn't feel natural, that doesn't feel restful, that doesn't feel conducive to a peaceful contented kind of life. Can you address that, please?

Yes, from the point of view of exclusive identification as the character, as the 'someone', there is the underlying intrinsic knowing of our true nature as wholeness, as being already complete. And it is the nature of the play that this apparent struggle as the individual takes place in order to try to return to wholeness. This struggle, and what appears as the search in many different forms—not just for so-called awakening or for wholeness, but for that which manifests as material gain, sexual fulfilment, earning a living, peace or whatever ... this struggle and search continues until there is the recognition of our true nature, or until this recognition begins at least to permeate into the play. Until then, the struggle as the individual tends to continue.

And so, initially, from the point of view of the individual, this message about our true nature permeating into the play doesn't seem to have much effect upon what is seen as the struggle of existence for the individual 'I'. However, if the character is continually moved to hear this reminder, then it is likely that there is a gradual unfolding of the recognition of wholeness, whereby ease is revealed. The tension—which we might liken to a wound-up spring, a clock mechanism—unwinds; it is gradually released. And in this ease, that which was previously seen from the point of view of the identified character as struggle, as all the difficulties of existence, of life, begins to be seen as simply a play.

So all of this unfolds as a play, and until knowing (which initially arose in the play as search and understanding) is revealed, the struggle of existence seems to continue—even when it is *understood* that it is just a struggle within the play. Which of course seems to be no consolation whatsoever to the identified character!

So it's back to work on Monday morning whether 'I' like it or not.

Yes.

Thank you very much! (laughter)

(Pause)

Can I bring Soggi to your next talk?

Who's Soggi?

She's my new pet rabbit. (laughter)

OK, why don't you bring your guinea pig as well, and hand out a few Avon catalogues while you're about it.

Well now you come to mention it ... (laughter)

East Sutton, Kent
One-Day Retreat

I've discovered as I've dropped so much of the seeking that now there's a tendency to think that I still have to have my attention on noticing that I'm aware, and that feels like a 'doing'. It seems very much as if you have to be aware of awareness for awareness to be there. Does that make sense?

There is already awareness, whether or not there is recognition of that—everything is already being registered. Usually this simple fact is overlooked in the exclusive identification with the content. When there is, in the play, the beginnings of this recognition, then it can seem like a struggle by the character to try to do something about being aware. This is the play: the permeation into the life of the apparent character of this initial seeing through of the story.

And you don't have to be noticing it for it to be occurring?

No, absolutely not. Without this registering, this awareness, there would be no appearance of the content.

So it's something that already *is*—not something that can be produced or found. It's already happening. There is already registering, and then there is this mesmerisation whereby a story arises that 'I' need to be aware of awareness. But in fact, as the mesmerisation is seen through, the struggle to be aware as the 'I' becomes obsolete. It naturally drops away.

So the only thing that is seen is the play, in all its vicissitudes. It's impossible to see what sees it.

Yes, what sees is what's doing the seeing, right now. What is seeing this body, seeing the wall, aware of these thoughts, aware of sensation?

So when the 'I' thought drops away, awareness can't be experienced because there is nothing to experience it.

No. Awareness is not an experience.

It just is, OK. So nothing at all arises of any kind, subtle or not subtle, that is not part of the play—nothing?

All that appears, all that arises, is the content being presently registered. That's all that is happening. And all attempts and ideas of struggling to be free of identification, to be aware of awareness, all of this is the play.

❋   ❋   ❋

We've been brought up with the idea that this 'I' must improve, but whether we behave well or badly or are selfish or not selfish or are kind or unkind, that's just really all the play of the played character. It's really got nothing at all to do with absolute truth. But as a character in a society, it does have importance if you don't realise that you're just a played character. It appears to have importance until the moment that it's seen.

Yes, but in the seeing, it's seen that 'you' are not just a 'played character'. Your true nature is oneness, so there is simply the present appearance of oneness *as* this character, *as* all that appears.

As the activities, even, of this character?

Yes, everything.

All the gentleness or the love or the violence or anything— it's just that, a play of appearances?

Oneness presently appears as all that is and there is no 'absolute truth', as you call it. This present appearance is it: the ordinariness of this roomful of characters.

The ordinariness of this roomful of characters is the content of awareness and that's it—there's no more to see?

No, nothing more at all. It's very simple. There is simply the content of awareness, presently. Very simple. All the rest of it is immersion in the thought story. It's so simple—so obvious—that it's overlooked. Awareness and presently appearing content, oneness ... what could be simpler?

We get tied up in all the whys and the wherefores and how we've got to know this and we've got to understand that, and we watch TV and see all those horrible programmes about violence and nasty things ... We think, 'This ought not to be,' or 'Why don't they do so and so?' And we tie ourselves up into terrible knots. It's not very easy to simply stand back from that. How do you see that just as part of the play?

There's no need for standing back. At times in the play as the character there will be the remembering of our true nature, and at times there will be forgetting. The whole of this struggle to make it work, to do the right thing, all the involvement with the daily news on the television—it's the story. The 'I' can't do anything about any of this; it cannot 'de-mesmerise' itself because it's part of the mesmerisation.

Maybe through this reminding of our true nature, or through the character in the play appearing to do some form of enquiry or whatever, the story, the play, is seen through. But this is not a prescription being made here—it's simply a description of what is. All prescriptions require the idea of identification as a separate character, and the idea that this supposedly separate character must do something to become whole.

So really, we can't do anything.

No, because the 'I' that would do something *is* the mesmerisation.

❋   ❋   ❋

Can we talk about memory? Thoughts that arise over and over again that appear to be a continuum, like 'I'm going to go home and cook supper for the family tonight'—they appear to be derived from memory.

'Memory' thoughts arise presently, and the content of these memory thoughts are the story of 'my' family.

So in presence there isn't a family unless they are present as actual physical images?

In presence there is whatever presently appears—what is. All else is the story.

OK. So when the family is present as actual physical images, why do these images seem familiar to me but other images—of strangers, say—don't? I can't seem to get away from the idea that the people, the characters that keep arising in one's story, apparently form a continuum.

In the appearance of the family images, there is an inbuilt sense of familiarity, a simultaneous 'memory' of the life that 'I' have led with 'my' family. There is no continuum—there is only presence. The whole history of 'my' family appears presently as a story.

What I find hard in that example is, OK, that is all appar-

ent here and the thoughts and the sensations are just lead-ing us to believe that that's the case—but what about the other person? How come they synchronise their sensations to exactly that same thing, 'Oh it's lovely to see you' or 'Oh God, not her again!' or whatever? They're having an experience which isn't dissimilar.

There is no synchronising on behalf of individual characters—it's all one complete whole, oneness. The appearance within and as oneness is of *seeming* sepa-ration. There is the present appearance of all of these images—the thoughts, the sensations, etc, all seem-ing to appear to corroborate each other for the play. That's the cosmic entertainment.

So that's God being very tricky indeed then.

There is no God apart from this present appearance. 'God' is not off in the background arranging it all but presently appearing *as* all of it.

But there does seem to be a synchronisation, doesn't there, in the play?

It appears that way, yes.

What I'm saying is, it's the other person's thought also. So it's like two people having that same thought, 'Oh it's nice to see you after twenty years.' How come it's the same thought?

With reference to the 'body of one' analogy—as in the

human body, everything is synchronised and simultaneous; everything is arising simultaneously. From the point of view of the individual cells or viewing points, from the point of view as the separate character, there is this play such that there is the appearance of there being 'other' separate characters. As in a movie, a character appears on the left and a character appears on the right, but they are both appearing in the one picture. Maybe the synchronicity of the play is puzzling from the apparently separate viewpoint of the identified character, but in actuality there is nothing but *total* synchronicity.

❀　　　❀　　　❀

Many years ago, I had an experience which lasted for three or four days in which everything was just the same as it ever had been—but it was also totally different. It was all beautiful and loving and very light—I can't put it into words really ... And then it went away. It seemed that this character re-entered the scene, or something of that sort.

Yes, with such a happening, the 'I' suddenly drops or is seen through. With this sudden dropping, the tension that arises with the 'I' story drops as well, which may feel like blissfulness or love. Whereas with a gradual recognising—in the play—of our true nature, there is simply a gentle relaxing into ease. It tends to be that where there is a sudden dropping of the 'I' then it likely reappears.

Yes. Because of the re-emergence of the 'I', there's been the desire to lose that 'I', to go back to that state of bliss. Which I suppose is an obstruction really, that desire.

Well, it's not actually an obstruction because there's no necessity to any of this, but within the play, it *appears* as an obstruction, because that very seeking itself *is* the inherent tension. It's the focus in the thought story, whereby presence is overlooked in focusing on the desire for this event to happen again in a projected future. There is the overlooking of presence through focus in the story.

Quite often when there is an event, the difficulty is with the bliss that comes with the clear seeing. The feeling itself is ascribed as being 'it'—liberation or enlightenment, whatever you want to call it—rather than the simple, ordinary clear seeing. There was a difficulty here about that for ages and ages.

Sure, yes. Because of the extremely compelling nature of this rush of blissfulness and …

… and the immense sense of love.

Yes, the awesomeness of it all. That is what is considered to be so-called enlightenment or awakening. Where this kind of an event is focused on as being significant in some way, then what is overlooked is that seeing is *already* happening. There is only already awakeness. There is no awakening to happen. This so-called awakening that is future-projected is, in fact, simply blissfulness or love or whatever, arising in the absence of the tension of seeking. Everything is already happening in this awakeness, whether it's suffering or bliss.

What is focusing on the present?

There is registering—or awareness—of what presently appears. The awareness *and* the appearances are presence. 'Focus' is used in the sense that there is awareness of the appearances without simultaneous recognition of the awareness aspect. So there is an *exclusive* focus on the images. This is the mesmerising or *maya*. *No-thing* is focusing.

But you're saying awareness is being overlooked. What do you mean by that?

Awareness is not being overlooked in the sense of it being some 'thing' that may be viewed or seen—rather, where there is exclusive focus in the content aspect, there is not simultaneous acknowledgement or recognition that there is awareness whereby everything is appearing. This simple recognition that there is awareness *and* the content of awareness is what is referred to as *seeing* or *knowing*. Knowing is not identification with content only, but abiding as awareness and content, without the subject-object sense. This is oneness or presence.

Can't there be an identification with the awareness aspect?

Yes. As part of the play there may be exclusive identification as awareness, whereby the content of awareness is viewed detachedly. And this tends to be the goal of traditional-type spirituality: get up and out the top of your head as quickly as possible! Escape the content into the awareness aspect.

Is this not about escaping from the content?

Our true nature is oneness: awareness *and* content. No escape is possible or needed
.

But what is different?

When the mesmerisation with the story is seen through, the contraction of tension and seeking is released. There is ease—no desire for escape.

So when we talk of an ease, we are not actually talking about emotions etc. disappearing? It's not that emotions don't still occur?

This ease may include the same pattern of appearances, but there is no longer the movement to escape from them. They are no longer 'my' emotions, 'my' thoughts etc.

I don't see how you can be angry and have lack of tension. I mean, if I'm furious because the pasta has boiled over and I've got a mess to clear up—well, I'm furious because it's happened! I'm furious because I allowed it to happen. I think 'What a fool!' We can hardly call that ease, can we? How could there be ease?

180

So when the pasta boils over, then maybe there is mesmerisation with content as the 'I' that has somehow 'allowed' the saucepan to boil over. It's the seeing of this 'I' for what it is—an appearance amongst all other appearances—that is the absence of mesmerisation, the absence of exclusive identification with the content aspect. There can be the pasta boiling over and the taking it off the stove and the mopping up of the stove or whatever is required, with no agitation around it.

So the story's still there but the tension is gone?

Yes, the story is no longer 'my' story. There is still the location as the character, but it's no longer 'my' body, 'my' story, although it's lived in that way ... It's seen through.

In that seeing that it's not 'mine', then there's a letting go of whatever.

There's never anyone to let go. It's simply that ease is revealed in the absence of the tension that appears along with the 'I'.

That tension seems like a holding on, doesn't it?

Yes, while it appears it seems like a grasping, a contraction.

So the difference between 'It's seen through' and 'It's not seen through'—it's nothing, and yet it's a hell of a difference.

It appears that way, yes. But in the play of life whereby there is a *gradual* seeing through the story and the revelation of ease, then it doesn't manifest as some big 'wow!' event.

The hearing that nothing can be done can allow the seeing through to happen.

The seeing through is not dependent on any happening in the play, although it may appear that understanding arises in the story of the character prior to *knowing* being revealed. But in the play, nonetheless, understanding may appear to have a profoundly relaxing effect, even *as* the character.

But when there is identification, understanding is no more valuable than not understanding.

No. Nothing is more valuable than anything else. If understanding is the apparent trigger that seems within the play to 'lead to' recognition, then that's the way it is for that character. But there's no kind of understanding needed whatsoever, because knowing simply permeates into the play. It doesn't require any process of seeking and understanding. That's all the play of appearances.

But when there's seeing, or knowing, agitation can still arise in that.

Yes.

The idea that that is the end of agitation—absolutely not.

Agitation may still arise, but there's a tendency for it to subside fairly quickly. There is no longer the story of this 'I' that it can 'stick to'.

In my understanding of all of this, there's a suggestion that when realisation that one is awake takes place, nothing changes.

There is only already awakeness whether there is mesmerisation in the thought story or not, so no appearances need to change. There is simply ease in the absence of mesmerisation. There may seem to be no difference, because there has been the story of gradual understanding which finally dissolves in knowing. Understanding may be described as the reflection of knowing in thought form.

The reflection of knowing in thought form?

Understanding is in thought, and as such is merely the 'reflection' of knowing. Knowing is simply what is, with no need for understanding. As knowing permeates the play and understanding becomes obsolete, there's not necessarily a clearly defined differentiation between them. In the play there's the gradual unwinding of the spring, the gradual relaxing of the tension (even with understanding as the 'I'), so that no clear definition is noticed between understanding and knowing. This is what is meant by permeation. There is no 'final' moment.

In the case of another character, it could be that there is some kind of a sudden dropping. With another character still, there could be a partial unwinding and *then* a sudden dropping. Or it could be that there is this gradual, gradual permeation, so that it seems that there's no 'difference' whatsoever.

Even where there is a sudden dropping with a big 'wow!' factor, that levels out anyway.

Yes, even in those cases where there is a sudden dropping and a big 'wow!'—a big rush of bliss and love and all the rest of it—that levels out and becomes the ordinary instead of being the extraordinary. What is sought as the extraordinary is actually here already, merely veiled by mesmerisation.

There's a concept I've heard about walking around with a stone in your shoe, this constant little niggling stone in your shoe. One day it just falls out and you feel, 'Ah, that's better!'

Yes, that's a nice analogy.

❀　　　❀　　　❀

All I want to know is, after the self falls away, is sex any different?

There is no after or before. This is the future-projected event again—and maybe hoping that when the 'I' is seen through then sex is going to be absolutely fantastic!　*(laughter)*

When you were talking about there being ease underlying agitation, I was just curious about other aspects of life, if there's ease underneath those too.

This ease is always the case: it's simply covered up by tension arising with mesmerisation. And so, in the absence of that tension, there is still this apparent life as the character, but it's no longer 'my' life. And in each case it's going to be different. The character may not have an active sex life. Or the character may be having a comfortable sex life or an uncomfortable sex life or a great sex life. Whatever is the content of the life of the character is unimportant stuff. Only from the point of view of the identified character, where there is seeking to be rid of this tension, are results looked for; the cause and effect thing. 'When there is liberation, then sex will be great.' There is presently 'what is', whether we stick a 'great' label on it or a 'mediocre' label.

❋　　　❋　　　❋

Nathan, what can't I accept about this story?

'You' can't accept or not accept anything.

OK, but some of what you say I can sort of understand. There is an understanding that all there is, is awareness and the content of awareness.

Yes.

And I can get that far, but I can't get this idea about a story. That's the thing that I'm really struggling with. Is it because I am coming from a place of 'I', I'm identified with this 'I' character? Is that what's getting in the way for me?

There is simply an overlooking of the awareness aspect of oneness such that there is exclusive focus in the thought story. And as a part of this thought story, there is the understanding of these concepts of awareness and content but, presently, there is not the relaxing into knowing.

Understanding is the reflection in thought of knowing. It's not anything that 'you', the character, are doing or not doing, because this character that you are taking yourself to be is in fact an appearance only. There is already, in the case of your character, a registering—oneness in its aspects of awareness and the content of awareness. There is already registering and there is the content, but there is exclusive identification as the content, and the registering, the awareness aspect, is being overlooked. It is understood, but because understanding is in thought, it appears and disappears—as do all appearances. When there is exclusive identification as the content, this story of the struggling character is taken to be real.

I'm wondering whether when there is an understanding or a knowing that the person is unreal, is there automatically also a knowing that other apparent persons are equally unreal? They get put together at the same time, as it were?

186

There's no need to say that the images are unreal—they are simply presently appearing images. And there's no longer the whole story of it extending into past and future, all relating to a central 'me' or an 'I'. So the images continue to appear but there's no longer the mesmerisation whereby the focus in the thought story is taken to be real.

So a lot of concepts can drop away spontaneously in an 'event'?

Yes, that may happen, and it's also possible that they may reappear. Or that there is, within the play of life, the story of the concepts gradually falling away as knowing gently permeates. Any scenario is possible.

But in whatever way the self is revealed to be unreal, whether it's sudden or whether it's gradual, then the unreality of all selves is also revealed?

The psychological self-sense is revealed to be a phantom, not an *entity* that is the natural partner of this bodily image. So all is seen to be a play of images—whether they are labelled 'real' or 'unreal'—including all apparent others. There is only Self (capital S), which is the registering and appearance of all 'selves'.

So with the seeing through of the psychological self-sense, everything is seen through in a way.

Yes. The whole of the story is constantly pointing to the seeing through of the story.

But that can only come about with the seeing through of the apparent self that's experiencing the story.

Yes, that's right—the recognition of oneness by oneness via the story in the play. There is no need, of course, for this story to appear. There is no need for oneness to recognise itself as oneness via the story in the play. It's simply the cosmic entertainment.

And memories are ghosts of the real stuff?

Memories are presently arising thoughts with a label on them—'memory thoughts'—which appear to contain pictures or stories of this character or other characters in the 'past'. The past is a story being viewed presently.

And part of that message is, 'This belongs to "me".'

Yes. There is an extension 'out of' presence into apparent time: past and future. 'My' past, 'my' future.

And that's what gives the story of the character apparent reality?

Yes.

Is this mesmerisation in the body-mind?

There's no mesmerisation *in* this body-mind—there is no body-mind as a complete and separate entity. There is simply the appearance of this body image and the thought images and the sensations and all the rest of it to which you're giving the label of 'body-mind'.

I'm still holding this ...

'You' are not doing anything.

OK, Consciousness, whatever, is still maintaining this apparent body-mind here by asking the question of that apparent body-mind, which supports the belief in these 'someones'. And that gets perpetuated and perpetuated.

That's the way it appears—the story. Whereas in fact there is no perpetuation as such—there is only presence. And inherent in this presently appearing story, there is the idea that it is being sustained or perpetuated in time.

That's the mystery bit, the elusive bit, you know: there's this here ... and later on this is going to be somewhere else ... and this here seems to be directing a question over there about, 'Is this really here?'

It's a very compelling story, isn't it?

Yeah.

❀   ❀   ❀

Can you say something about what we were talking about in the kitchen—the eating of the ice cream? How can it be that I can eat half a litre of ice cream and you can't? That you can't—or that physical body can't—seems to imply that that body is different from this one.

Consciousness or oneness is presently appearing as every character and that's the spice of the story, that one character can eat half a litre of ice cream and the other character has trouble digesting a spoonful.

What does that say about the physical body—does that make this body 'real' then?

All that appears presently are images, whether we label them real or unreal.

But the eating of ice cream seems to be a physical thing—a material thing called ice cream that goes into this material thing called a body. Those are just images? And the ice cream is images?

Yes.

How can there be this different effect?

This is the play of appearances. So there is an image of eating a half-litre of ice cream and there is an image of eating a spoonful of ice cream. What's the problem?

No problem, as I'm the one eating the half-litre!

Damn! (*laughter*)

OK, so I'm looking at Nathan and thinking, 'If tension

has gone or the spring has unwound and all of that' … I suppose it doesn't fit my idea of this image where if those things have happened, you could eat whatever.

Sure, this idea of the so-called 'enlightened man'—you imagine this spunky great character striding across the Himalayas with staff in hand spontaneously creating lightning and all the rest of it. But that's just a story.

We love to see our teachers in robes and drama. We can't stand it if they are as ordinary as we are.

Sure. But actually there is only this play of presently arising images, and it appears, in the case of some of these images, that there is the expression of the direct pointing to our true nature. There is no significance to any of that; there is no advantage to any of it at all. There is only oneness, only already awakeness; Consciousness appearing immanently as everything.

The play seems concrete, it seems real, and so it seems to reinforce the idea that there's a difference between the characters.

There is only oneness which includes all appearances, and all of these appearances seem different. That's the play. Oneness appears presently as each character with a different story running. And maybe the story is seen through and maybe not.

Is it just because we don't surrender into oneness that we go on chipping away at this?

'You' can't surrender. What is going to surrender?

Well, it seems so obvious what you're saying, when you're saying it, and I think, 'Oh yes, of course! It's obvious.' And yet all round the room, we're chipping at the story one way or another rather than just resting in oneness.

Well, that's the nature of this little scene in the play: this constant chipping away and undermining of the exclusive focus as content. And maybe understanding appears, which is the initial permeating into the play of knowing. Then maybe understanding dissolves in knowing.

Nathan, can I just say that I used to be strongly addicted to the idea that surrender was the answer and the dropping of the 'me' was the answer. And I chased Nathan and Tony and various others who were talking a lot about the 'me' dropping and all of that. But none of it is actually the answer.

Sure yes, all of it is the story. There is no final answer.

When that's realised, surrender happens. So surrender's not the answer, but when it's seen that it's not the answer, it happens.

An apparent surrendering happens, but there is no one that surrenders. This surrendering is another term for seeing through the 'I', but it tends to be misleading because of its traditional connotations—seemingly referring to an 'I' that can surrender.

OK.

Well, I guess that's about it for today.

How quickly it's gone...
                        (unintelligible comment & laughter)
What was that?

She said, 'It hasn't gone quickly—it was torture!'
(*laughter*)

Bless you all.

East Sutton, Kent

'Captain' Scott Drops In

It's interesting that, when this play of seeking enlightenment or awakening first arises, there's a focus on looking for a big hit—all the cosmic fireworks. But as the play unfolds, this search for the fireworks is undermined by the emergence of ease or peace, rather, as our true nature is revealed.

Yes, it could be realised in one hit or gradually, that there's no escape. Whichever way, it simply relaxes.

I remember when we first met, you came to a talk and there was a real intensity going on there.

Yeah, don't remind me! (laughter)

There was always the nagging little frustration that I—or 'who I thought I was'—always had to do something for a constant sense of oneness to be there all the time. Even if it was to hear that there was nothing to do, or to just hang at the meetings, or to hang with Nathan or Tony or whoever it was that I needed to be with. That was the focus for what was sought as awakening. And it was only seeing through this idea of 'who I thought I was' that kind of undermined that whole movement, the anticipation and waiting around for something to happen.

In the drama of seeking it tends to be that if the focus isn't on looking for a big hit, then it's on looking for a continual state of whatever is perceived as enlightenment.

A felt sense of oneness is often the goal. That's certainly how it appeared here.

It seemed in your case there was particular significance in the recognition of the futility of asking the questions—the recognition that the questions, in fact, don't end in some big answer.

Yes. But the questions always came out of the idea that there is a final answer. It was only when there was the seeing that the final answer is that there is no final answer, and that being is infinitely, forever ongoing—there is never any end, that it could relax. The focus in thought could relax and hence the seeking. Because the idea that the final answer was still yet to come somehow reinforced the idea that there was still 'someone' there to get the answer. So as you've said, to keep hearing this over and over and over—that there is no final place to land, that this present unfolding is all there is—allows the resting.

There's no final answer—simply this present openness.

Without there being any idea of there being any more or any less than whatever it is.

Yes, the tension that arises in conjunction with focus on the thought story is the root of seeking, which, in the play of life, is often translated as the search for more. 'What is' is never enough!

Right, but there's no ending of seeking until it naturally drops, until it's seen for what it is. And that can only happen when it happens.

The story running with the seeking, of course, is that there will be some advantage or something to be gained at the end of it.

Yes, which is conceptualised and turned into an object of desire. Whatever way we say it—even if we say 'It's a non-event'—then it becomes, 'Ah, the non-event will give me the buzz!'

The non-event becomes—the event! (*laughter*)

It's crazy because the seeker is only ever an imaginary 'someone' projecting an imaginary answer. Consciousness appearing as everything, playing the whole game, experiencing itself as all of these various forms.

From the point of view of this play of seeking, what seems to be important, in the unfolding of the talks, is that at first a character turns up at the talks, looking for what is perceived as enlightenment or awakening, some future projected event. So initially these concepts of Consciousness (with its aspects of awareness and the content of awareness) appear useful. With this constant reminding of our true nature, the 'I' is seen for what it is and the search begins to collapse. Rather than the search for the extraordinary, there is a collapse into the ordinary—but without the tension of seeking. The 'I' is seen through and an ordinary life is lived. And all of this—which before seemed so profound, the whole seeking for enlightenment drama—is just seen as a pile of cack. (*laughter*)

Simply another one of the infinite expressions. The one appearing as the many, looking for the one. In some cases, it may not be seen through.

That's right. It's only a play after all. There's no necessity to any of it.

So if it's going to be seen through, it will be seen through. Nothing can bring it about, nothing can avoid it.

Exactly, it's all on auto-pilot. Everything, including every thought that arises ... It's all automatic. With this seeing, the tension disappears from it all.

It takes 'me' and 'my' out of the whole equation, which—within the story in the play—seems to be the root of the whole drama, of all of the suffering. 'My' suffering and 'my' seeking and 'my' life. There was never an entity in the first place—it was only a phantom. Seeing through that idea is the root.

Within the whole seeking drama of the play, arising with this scene of seeking for awakening or enlightenment, there is the idea that this is some special, 'ultimate' kind of seeking; that *this* kind of seeking is more important or special than 'ordinary' seeking for a new car.

Yes, there seems to be a kind of arrogance or importance built into it, that 'spiritual' seeking is grand seeking, while your seeking—you plebs 'down there' seeking cars or whatever—is inferior. Whereas all seeking—the whole thing— is the one: 'what we really are' wanting to rest in 'what we really are'.

Already resting but appearing not to.

And so nothing ever happened. Nothing ever happened at all.

In the play there is an obsession with the importance of this: that there is going to be some special awakening or so-called enlightenment, that there's going to be something absolutely special about it. Of course, it's possible that there may be blissful experiences, and there is certainly an ease, the ease that is revealed in seeing the play for what it is. But it's not an ultimate event—it's simply the ease of being in the absence of the tension of seeking.

It's the peace that was always sought.

Yes, the peace which is sought—which is, in fact,

covered up by the seeking for peace. Something of a paradox.

And the peace is here without 'me' wanting it this way or that way, constantly seeking an advantage in having it this way and not that way. It's the 'me' ascribing meaning to the future event, because then 'I'—this 'me'—this 'I' thought, whatever we want to call it—will finally be free of all of 'my' suffering!

But no thought is ever going to be free of anything because a thought is just a thought. In the play, all sorts of characters appear, proclaiming enlightenment and blissfulness and events that have happened ... And this is the spice that has the appearance of keeping the seeking going.

Yes, unless there is the constant undermining of the 'I', then from the identified character's point of view, all talk of awakening, spiritual experiences, etc, reinforces the whole game and the idea of a future event. But from an absolute point of view, where there is the constant undermining of the 'I', then any idea of future events or of anything needing to be other than what it is is simply unnecessary. There is only Consciousness playing the whole game.

So as a play, the talking arises through the appearance of seekers asking questions, and it comes out the way it comes out. It couldn't come out any other way than it comes as Nathan or whoever. Of course there's no necessity at all for any of that to happen, but here it is happening.

As we've said, when the seeking drama collapses,

there is relaxing into an ordinary life, and all is simply as it is. The play continues but without the tension of seeking.

Infinitely unfolding in its expression as the particular character.

The character is seen through and yet there is still appearance *as* the character. What else is there to appear as?

(Pause)

Well, that's enough of that. Switch that tape off and we'll get down to the pub, Captain.

Sounds good to me, buddy, the drinks are on me.

It's been a creamy summer.

Yeah, nice one.

Other titles of interest from Non-Duality Press:

Nathan Gill
Being: the bottom line

Leo Hartong
Awakening to the Dream
From Self to Self

Richard Sylvester
I Hope You Die Soon

John Wheeler
Shining in Plain View
Awakening to the Natural State
Right Here, Right Now

'Sailor' Bob Adamson
What's Wrong with Right Now?
Presence-Awareness

John Greven
Oneness

David Carse
Perfect Brilliant Stillness

Joan Tollifson
Awake in the Heartland

CPSIA information can be obtained
at www.ICGtesting.com
Printed in the USA
FFOW03n0432071215
19187FF